HEY, PEANUTS!

Selected Cartoons From
MORE PEANUTS
Vol. 2

by Charles M. Schulz

A Fawcett Crest Book

Fawcett Publications, Inc., Greenwich, Conn.

Member of American Book Publishers Council, Inc.

This book, prepared especially for Fawcett Publications, Inc.,
comprises the second half ot MORE PEANUTS, and is
reprinted by arrangement with Holt, Rinehart and Winston, Inc.

Fifteenth Fawcett Crest printing May 1968

Published by Fawcett World Library,
67 West 44th Street, New York, N. Y. 10036
Printed in the United States of America

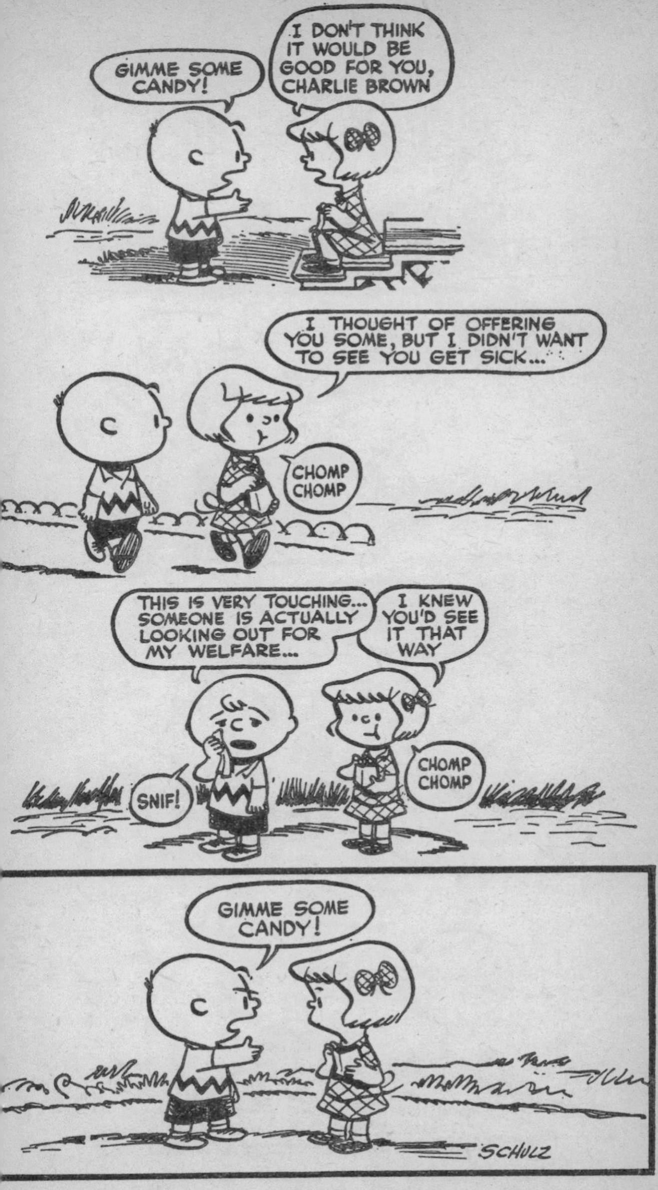
GIMME SOME CANDY!
I DON'T THINK IT WOULD BE GOOD FOR YOU, CHARLIE BROWN
I THOUGHT OF OFFERING YOU SOME, BUT I DIDN'T WANT TO SEE YOU GET SICK...
CHOMP CHOMP
THIS IS VERY TOUCHING... SOMEONE IS ACTUALLY LOOKING OUT FOR MY WELFARE...
I KNEW YOU'D SEE IT THAT WAY
SNIF!
CHOMP CHOMP
GIMME SOME CANDY!
SCHULZ

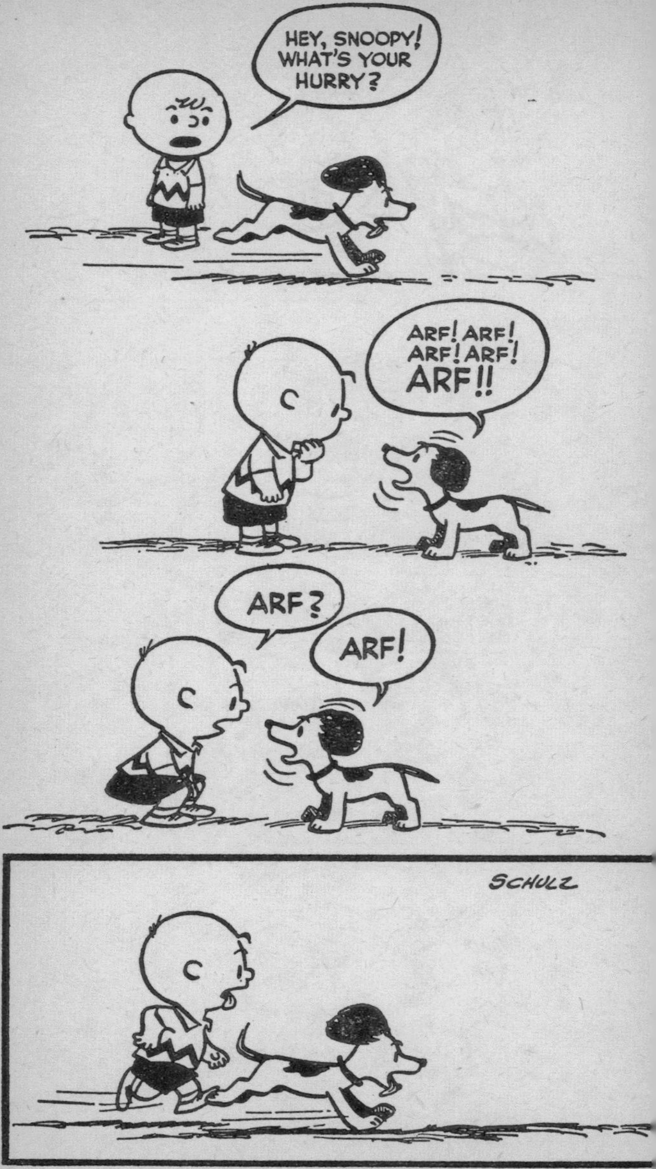
HEY, SNOOPY! WHAT'S YOUR HURRY?
ARF! ARF! ARF! ARF! ARF!!
ARF?
ARF!
SCHULZ

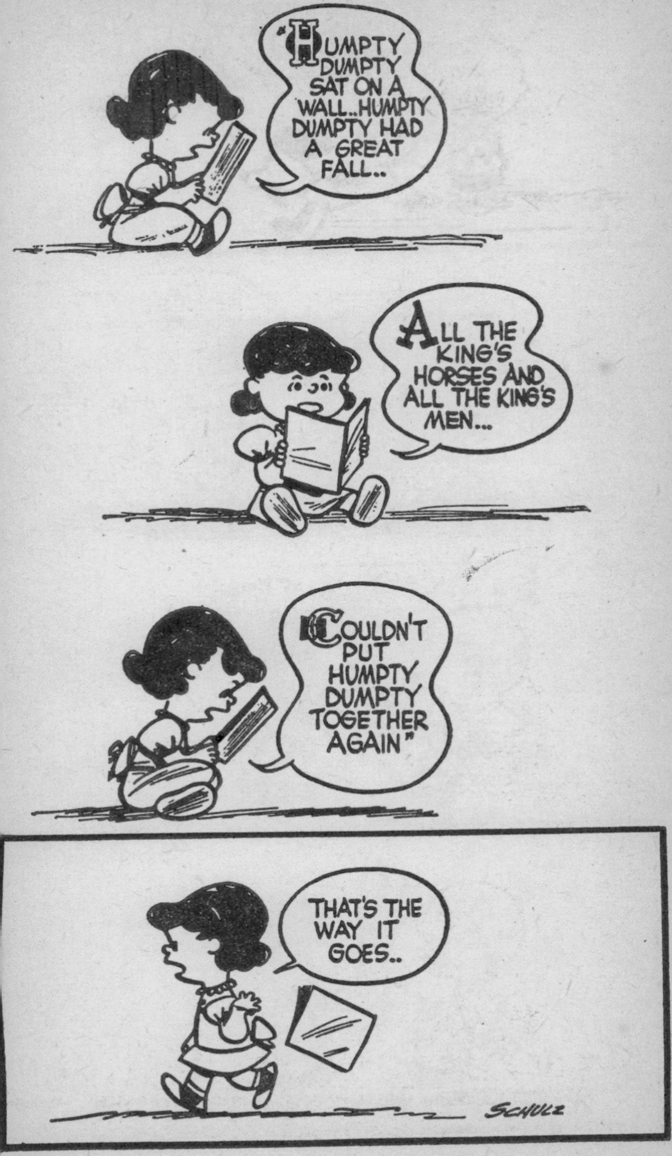
"HUMPTY DUMPTY SAT ON A WALL..HUMPTY DUMPTY HAD A GREAT FALL..
ALL THE KING'S HORSES AND ALL THE KING'S MEN...
COULDN'T PUT HUMPTY DUMPTY TOGETHER AGAIN"
THAT'S THE WAY IT GOES..
SCHULZ

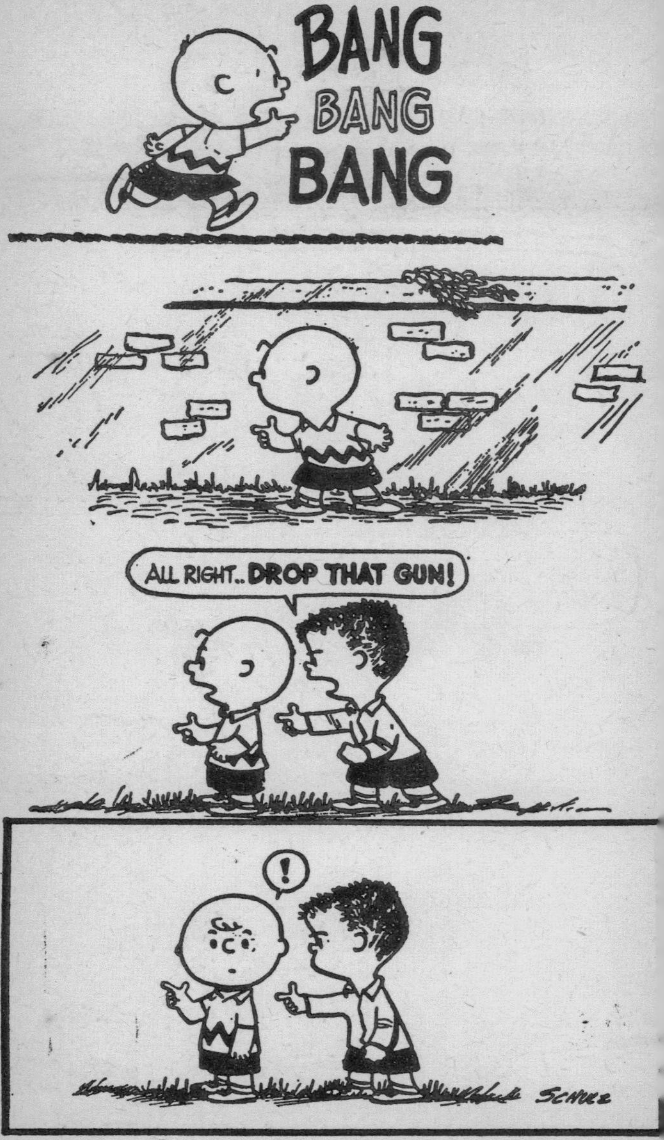
BANG
BANG
BANG
ALL RIGHT.. DROP THAT GUN!
!
SCHULZ

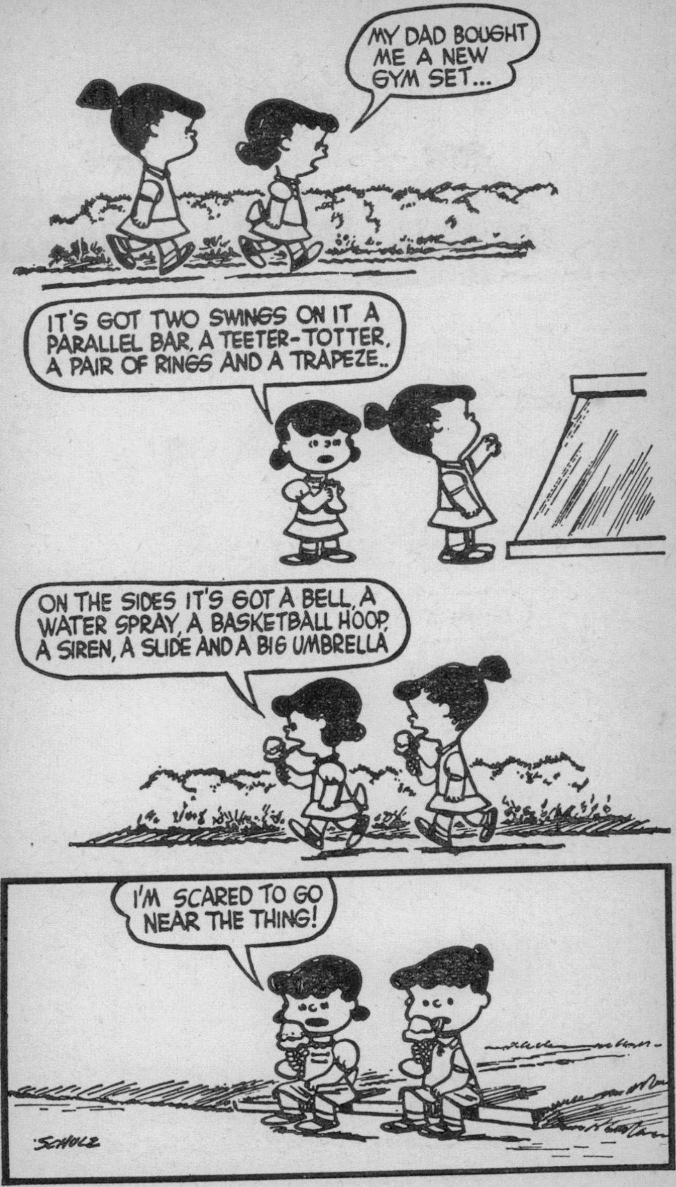
MY DAD BOUGHT ME A NEW GYM SET...
IT'S GOT TWO SWINGS ON IT A PARALLEL BAR, A TEETER-TOTTER, A PAIR OF RINGS AND A TRAPEZE..
ON THE SIDES IT'S GOT A BELL, A WATER SPRAY, A BASKETBALL HOOP, A SIREN, A SLIDE AND A BIG UMBRELLA
I'M SCARED TO GO NEAR THE THING!
SCHULZ

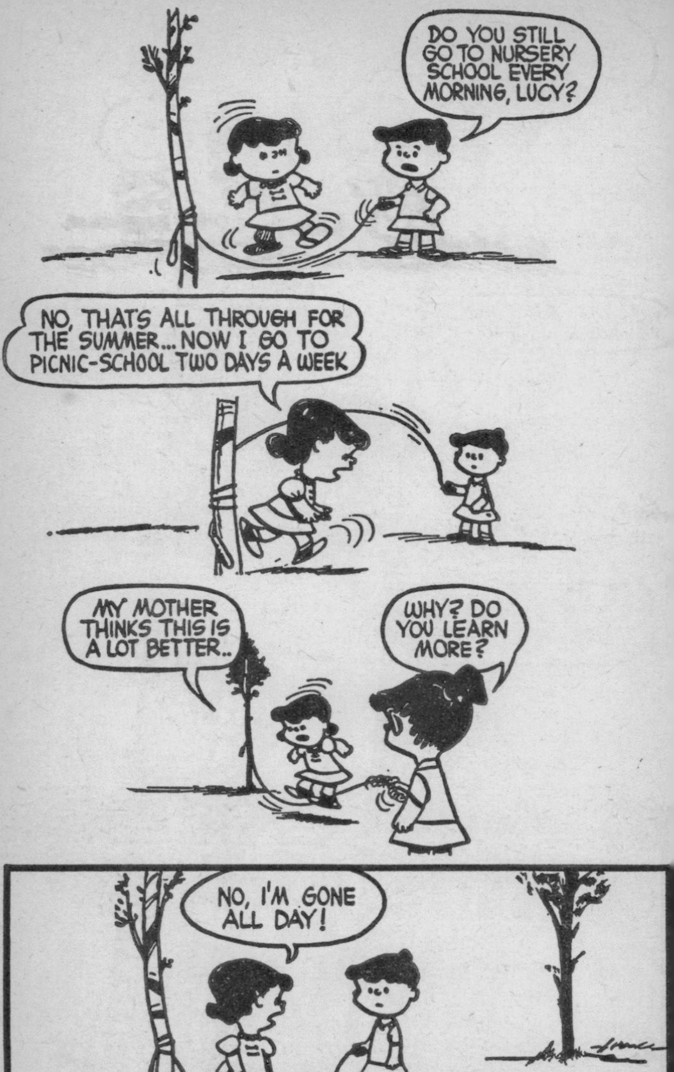
DO YOU STILL GO TO NURSERY SCHOOL EVERY MORNING, LUCY?
NO, THAT'S ALL THROUGH FOR THE SUMMER... NOW I GO TO PICNIC-SCHOOL TWO DAYS A WEEK
MY MOTHER THINKS THIS IS A LOT BETTER..
WHY? DO YOU LEARN MORE?
NO, I'M GONE ALL DAY!
SCHULZ

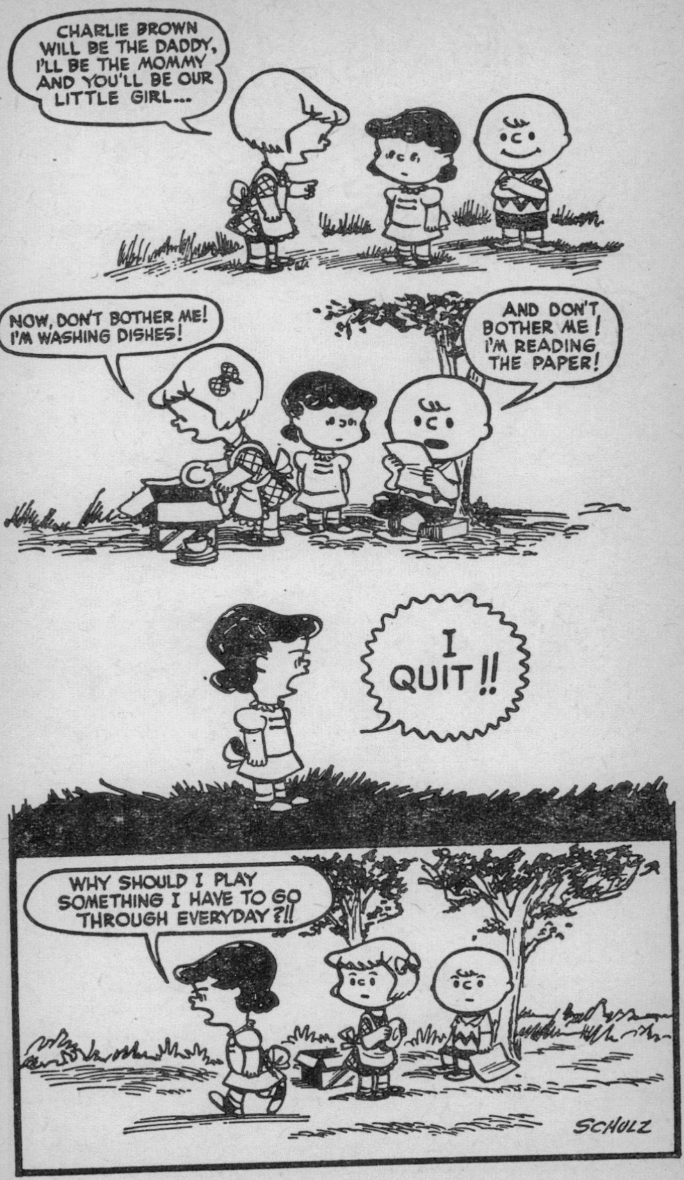
CHARLIE BROWN WILL BE THE DADDY, I'LL BE THE MOMMY AND YOU'LL BE OUR LITTLE GIRL...
NOW, DON'T BOTHER ME! I'M WASHING DISHES!
AND DON'T BOTHER ME! I'M READING THE PAPER!
I QUIT!!
WHY SHOULD I PLAY SOMETHING I HAVE TO GO THROUGH EVERYDAY?!!
SCHULZ

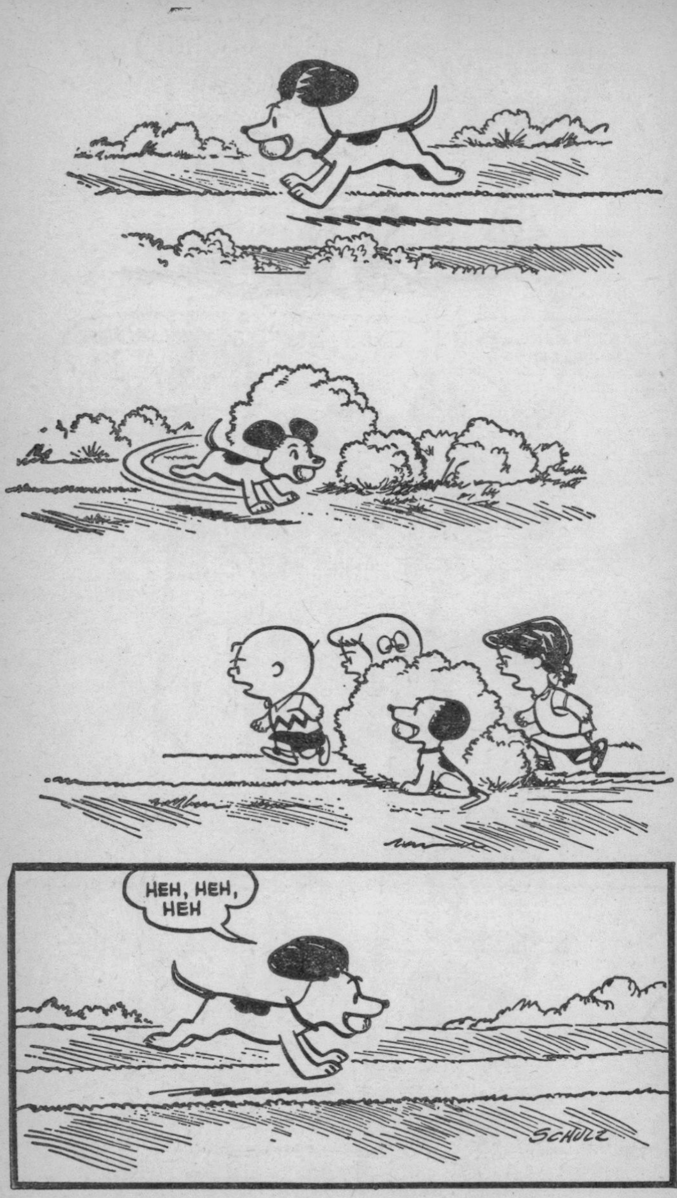
HEH, HEH, HEH
SCHULZ

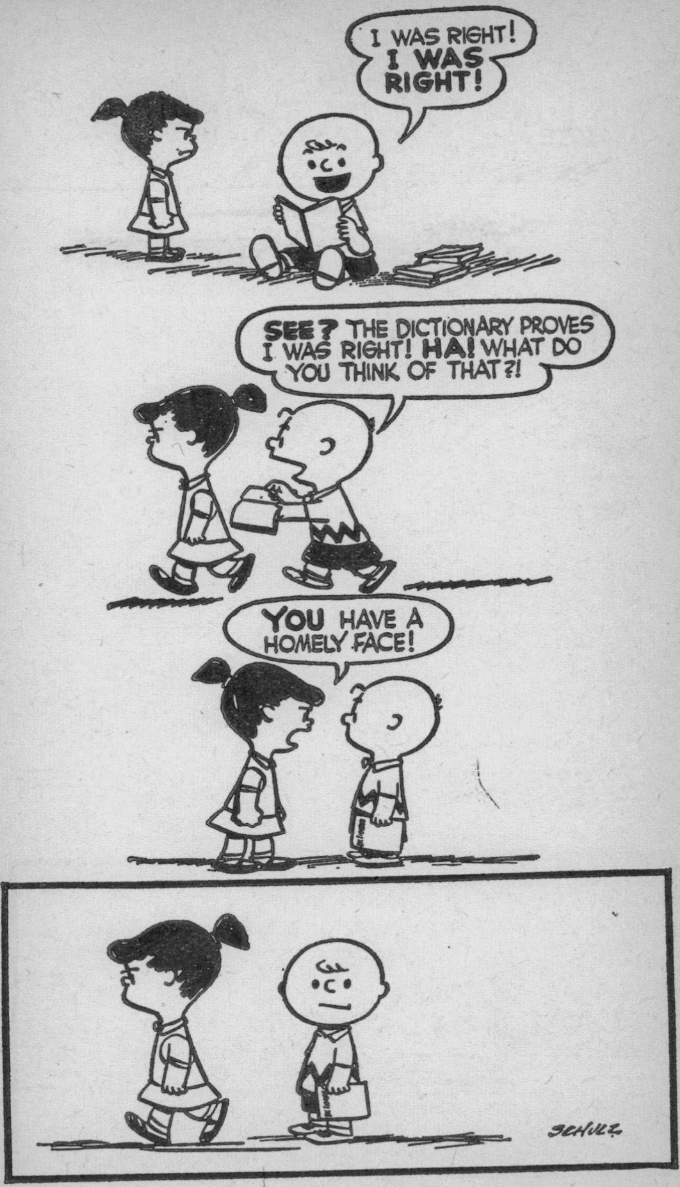
I WAS RIGHT! I WAS RIGHT!
SEE? THE DICTIONARY PROVES I WAS RIGHT! HA! WHAT DO YOU THINK OF THAT?!
YOU HAVE A HOMELY FACE!
SCHULZ

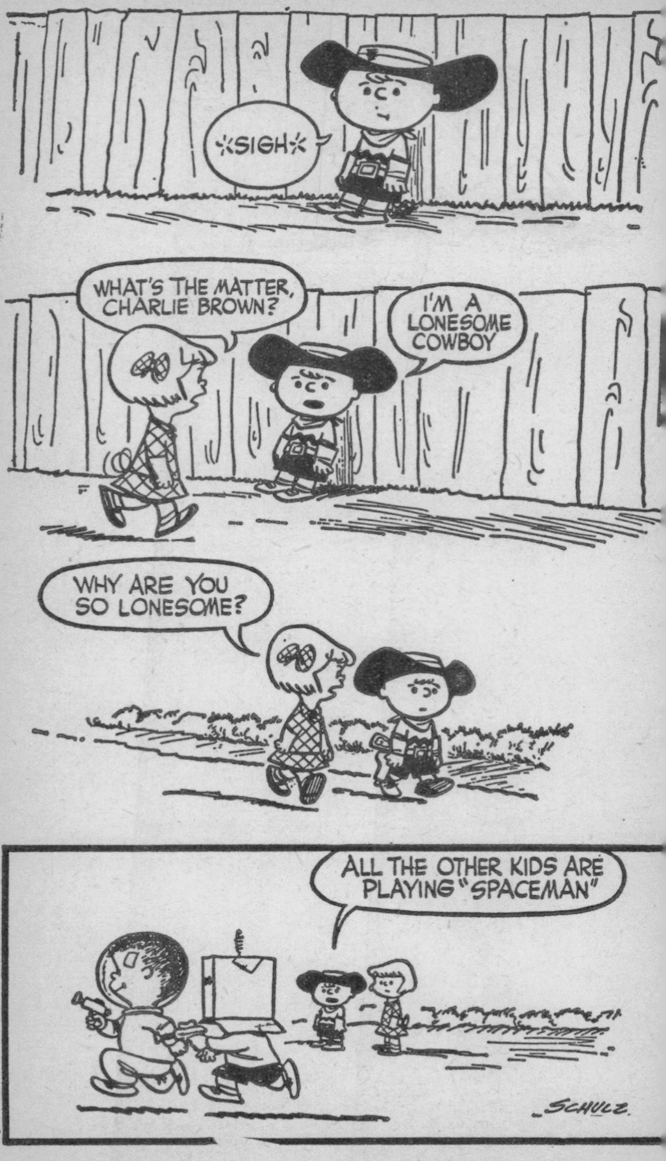

SIGH
WHAT'S THE MATTER, CHARLIE BROWN?
I'M A LONESOME COWBOY
WHY ARE YOU SO LONESOME?
ALL THE OTHER KIDS ARE PLAYING "SPACEMAN"
SCHULZ

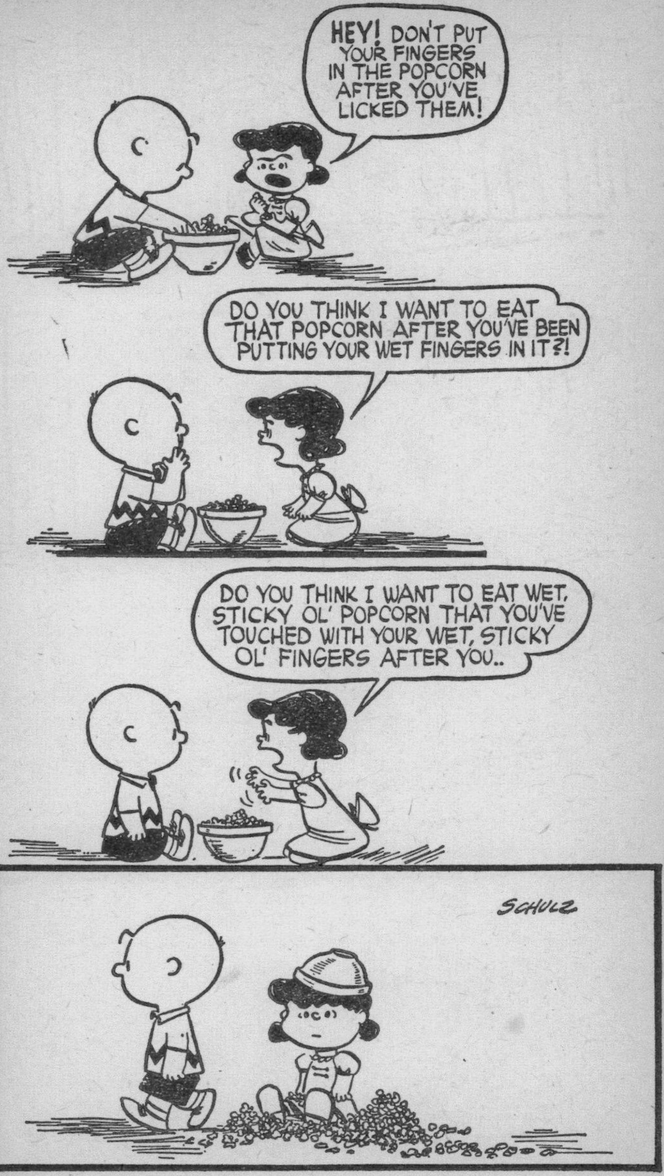
HEY! DON'T PUT YOUR FINGERS IN THE POPCORN AFTER YOU'VE LICKED THEM!
DO YOU THINK I WANT TO EAT THAT POPCORN AFTER YOU'VE BEEN PUTTING YOUR WET FINGERS IN IT?!
DO YOU THINK I WANT TO EAT WET, STICKY OL' POPCORN THAT YOU'VE TOUCHED WITH YOUR WET, STICKY OL' FINGERS AFTER YOU..
SCHULZ

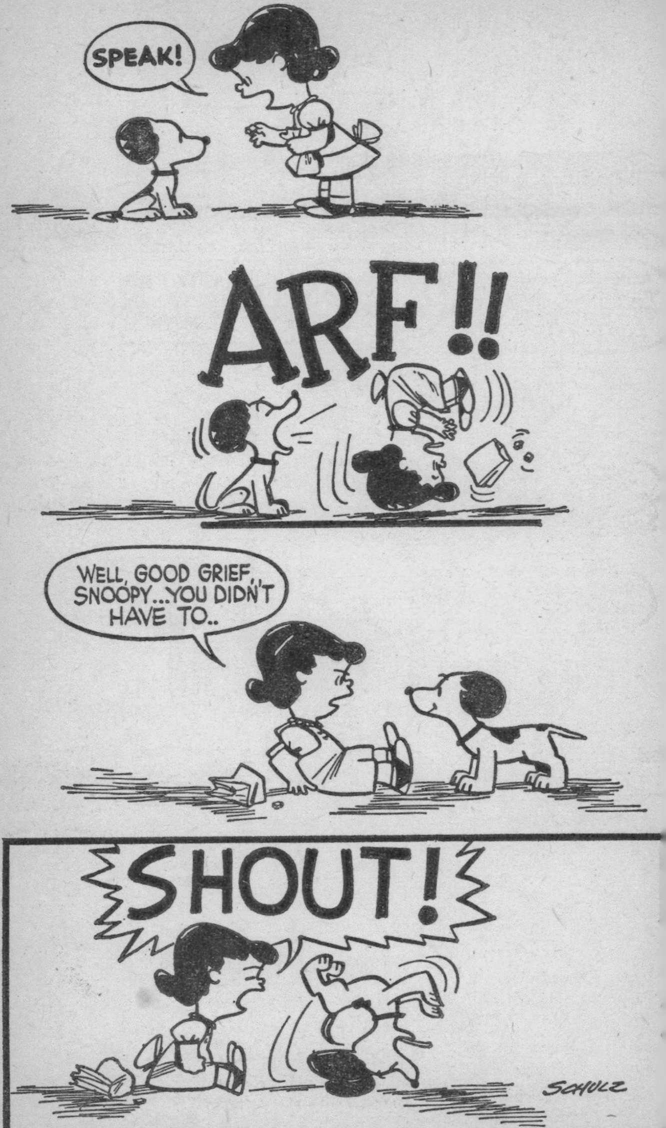
SPEAK!
ARF!!
WELL, GOOD GRIEF, SNOOPY...YOU DIDN'T HAVE TO..
SHOUT!
SCHULZ

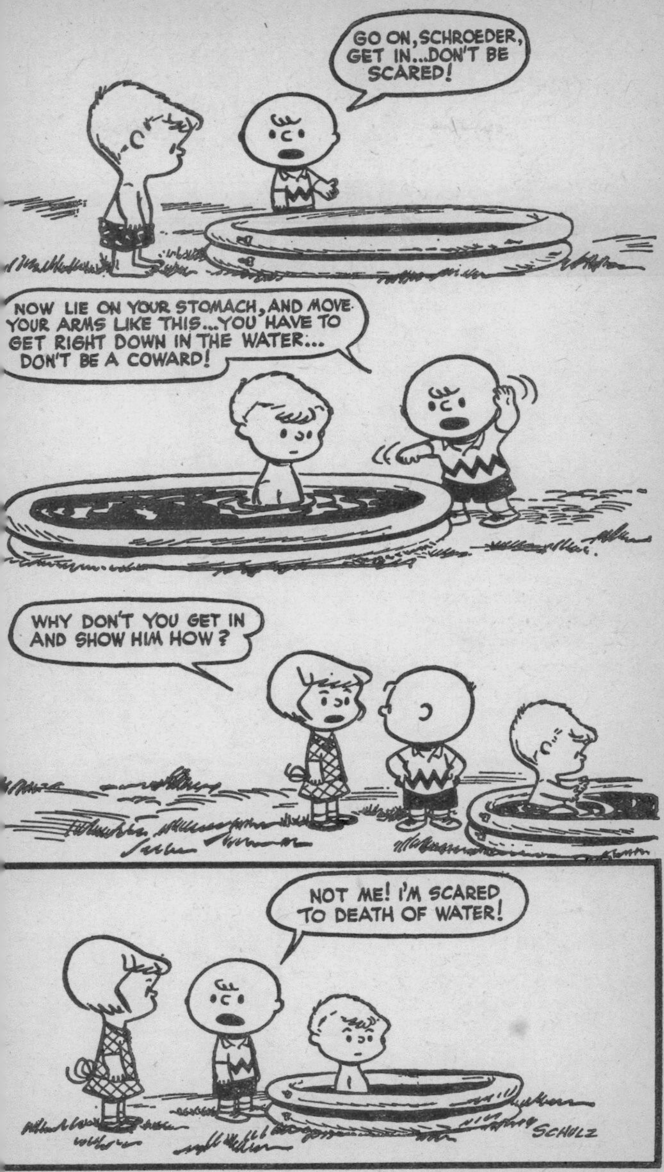
GO ON, SCHROEDER, GET IN...DON'T BE SCARED!
NOW LIE ON YOUR STOMACH, AND MOVE YOUR ARMS LIKE THIS...YOU HAVE TO GET RIGHT DOWN IN THE WATER... DON'T BE A COWARD!
WHY DON'T YOU GET IN AND SHOW HIM HOW?
NOT ME! I'M SCARED TO DEATH OF WATER!
SCHULZ

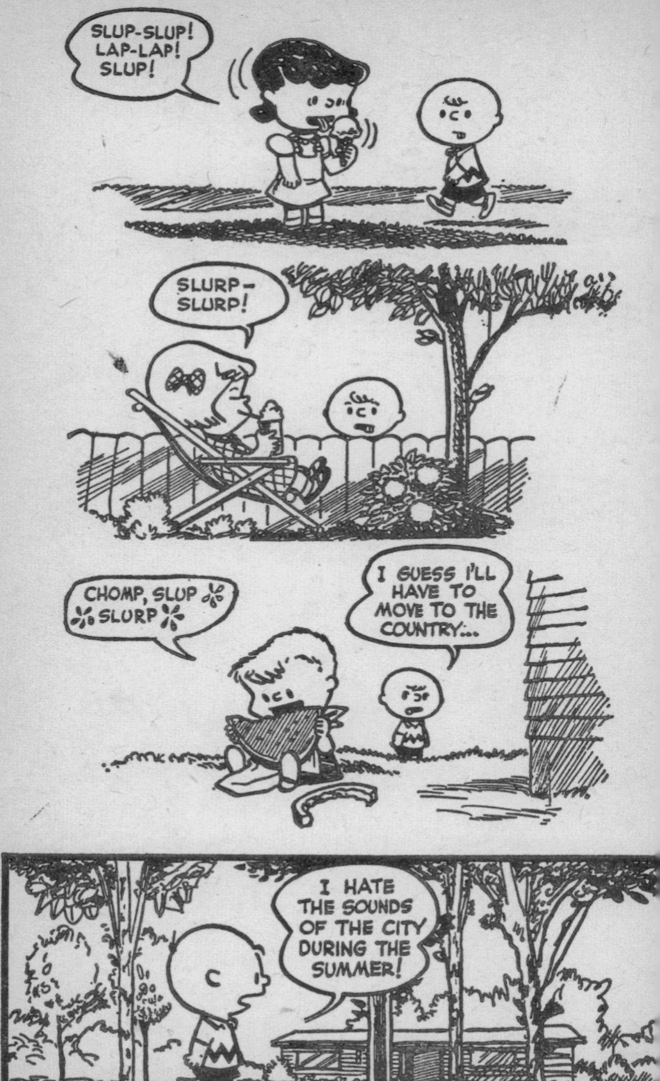
SLUP-SLUP! LAP-LAP! SLUP!
SLURP-SLURP!
CHOMP, SLUP SLURP
I GUESS I'LL HAVE TO MOVE TO THE COUNTRY...
I HATE THE SOUNDS OF THE CITY DURING THE SUMMER!
SCHULZ

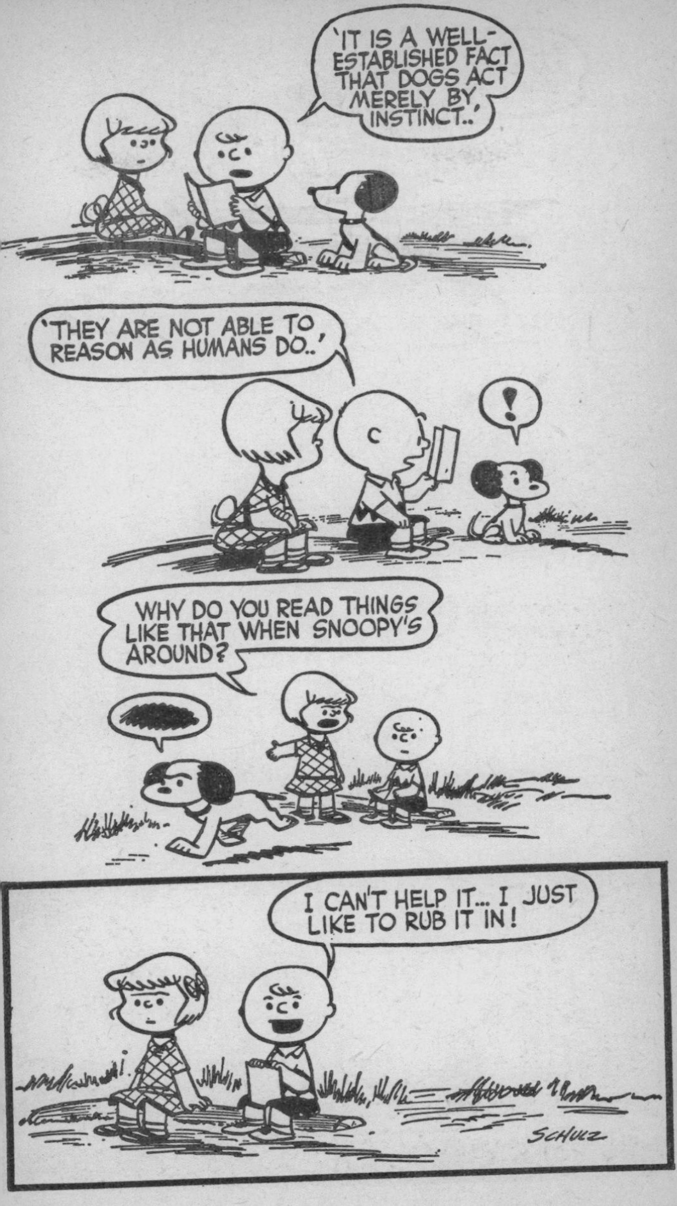
'IT IS A WELL-ESTABLISHED FACT THAT DOGS ACT MERELY BY INSTINCT..'
'THEY ARE NOT ABLE TO REASON AS HUMANS DO..'
!
WHY DO YOU READ THINGS LIKE THAT WHEN SNOOPY'S AROUND?
I CAN'T HELP IT... I JUST LIKE TO RUB IT IN!
SCHULZ

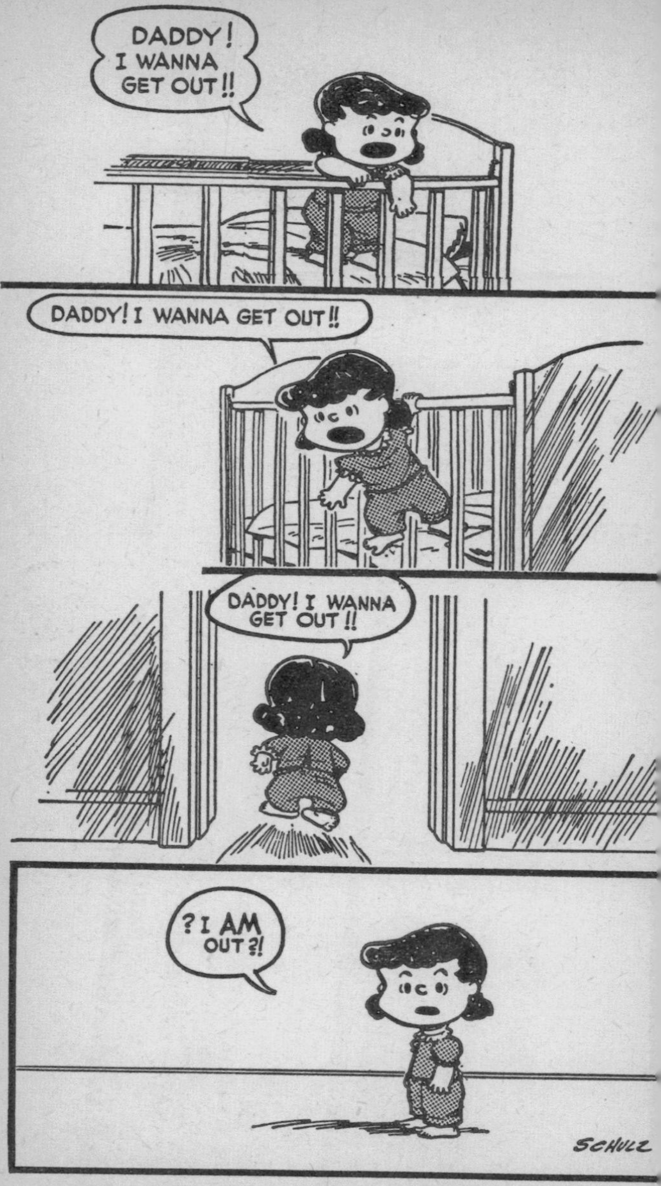
DADDY! I WANNA GET OUT!!
DADDY! I WANNA GET OUT!!
DADDY! I WANNA GET OUT!!
?I AM OUT?!
SCHULZ

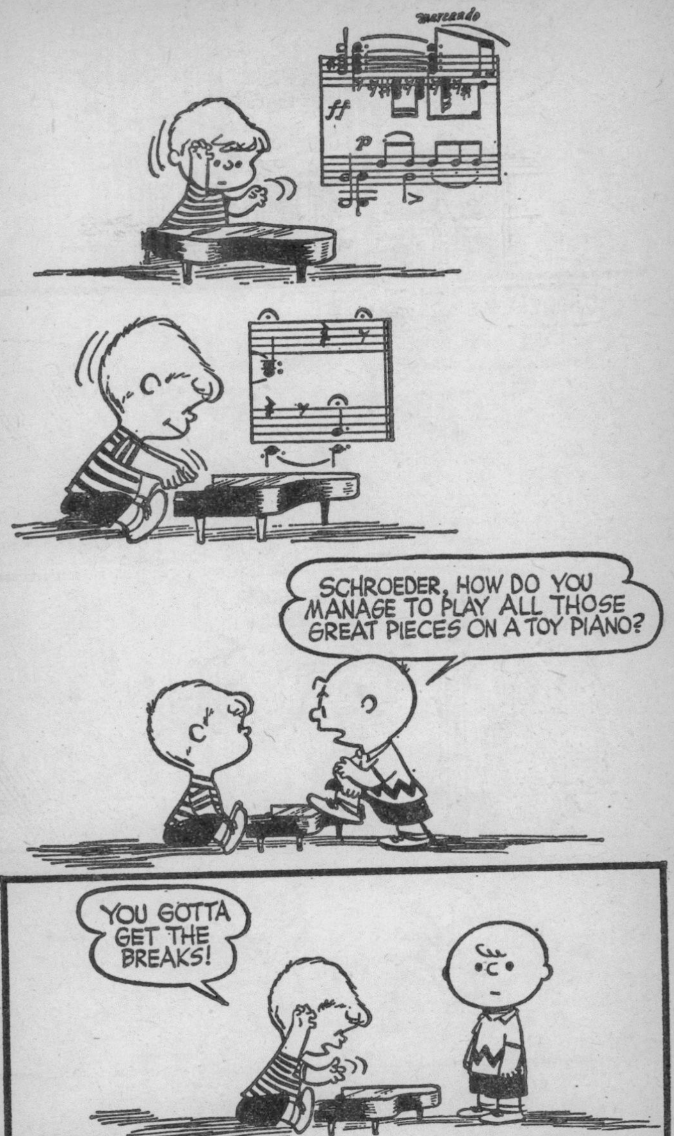
marcando
ff
p
SCHROEDER, HOW DO YOU MANAGE TO PLAY ALL THOSE GREAT PIECES ON A TOY PIANO?
YOU GOTTA GET THE BREAKS!
SCHULZ

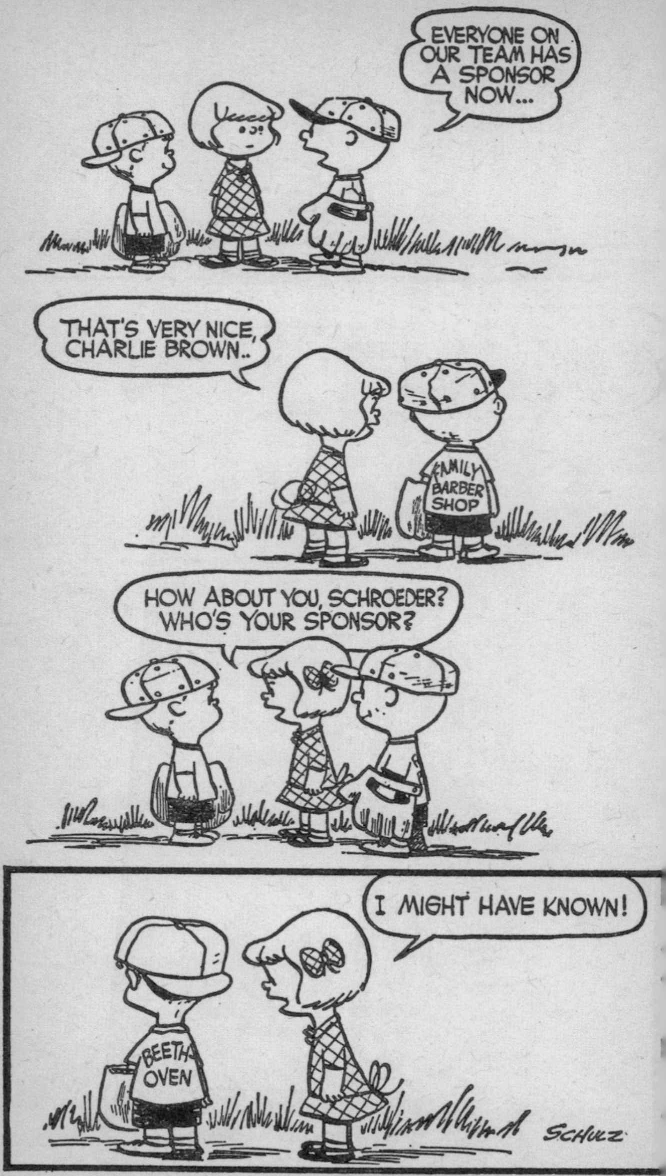
EVERYONE ON OUR TEAM HAS A SPONSOR NOW...
THAT'S VERY NICE, CHARLIE BROWN..
FAMILY BARBER SHOP
HOW ABOUT YOU, SCHROEDER? WHO'S YOUR SPONSOR?
I MIGHT HAVE KNOWN!
BEETH OVEN
SCHULZ

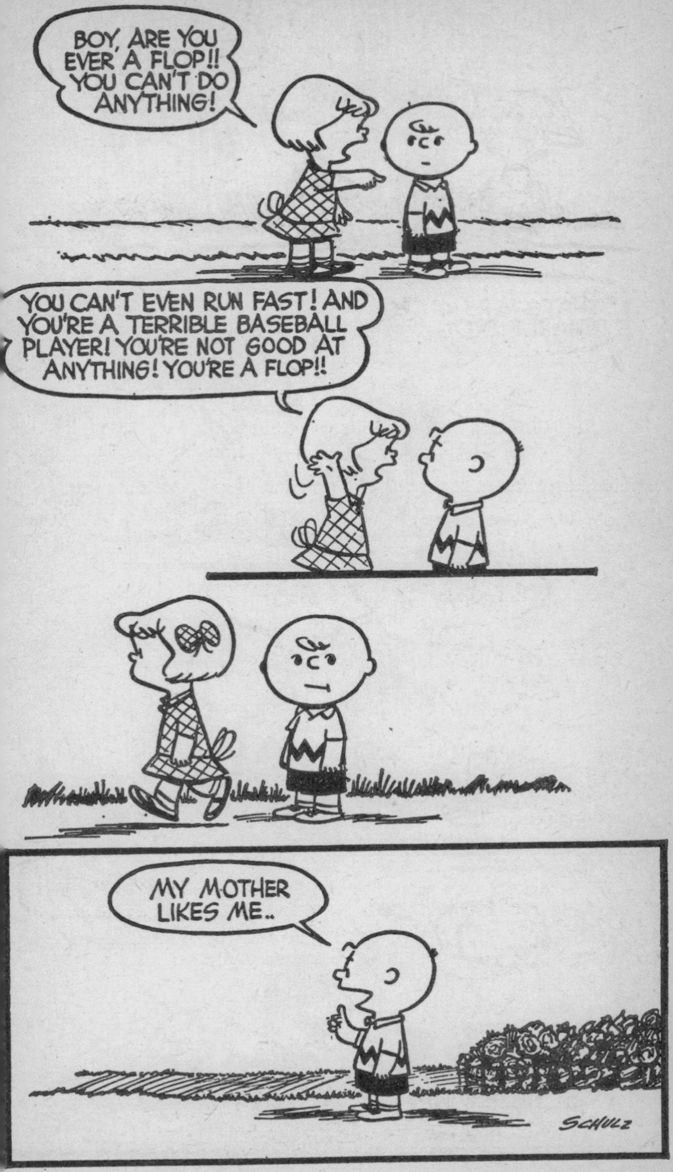
BOY, ARE YOU EVER A FLOP!! YOU CAN'T DO ANYTHING!
YOU CAN'T EVEN RUN FAST! AND YOU'RE A TERRIBLE BASEBALL PLAYER! YOU'RE NOT GOOD AT ANYTHING! YOU'RE A FLOP!!
MY MOTHER LIKES ME..
SCHULZ

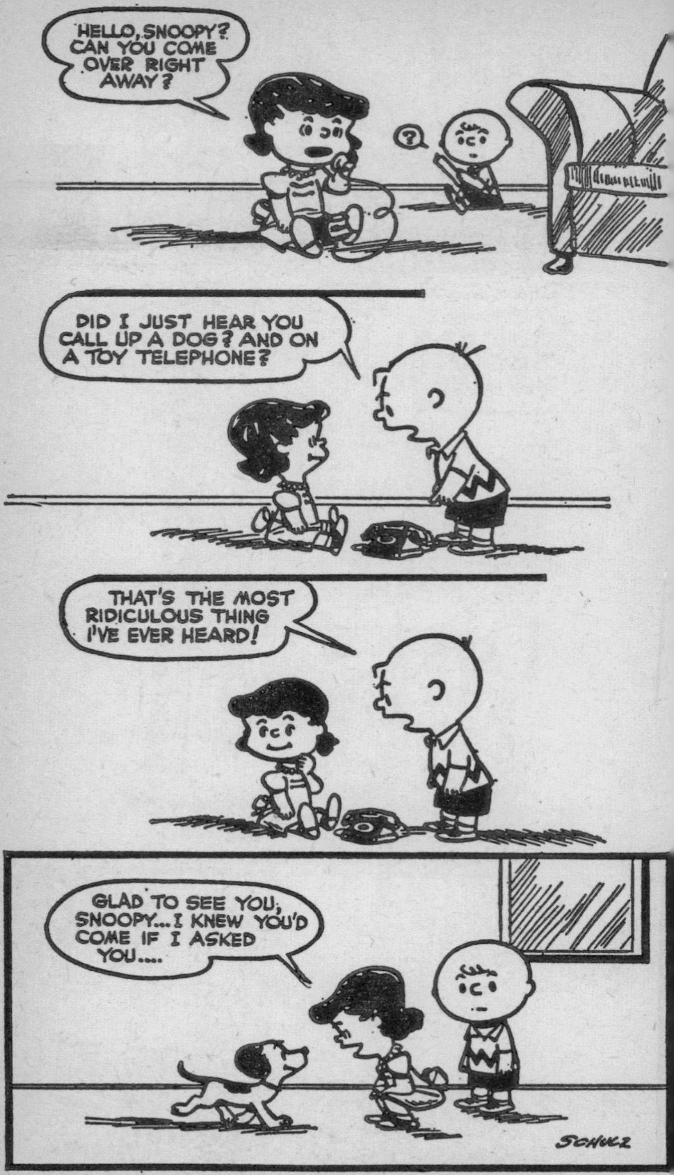
HELLO, SNOOPY? CAN YOU COME OVER RIGHT AWAY?
?
DID I JUST HEAR YOU CALL UP A DOG? AND ON A TOY TELEPHONE?
THAT'S THE MOST RIDICULOUS THING I'VE EVER HEARD!
GLAD TO SEE YOU, SNOOPY... I KNEW YOU'D COME IF I ASKED YOU....
SCHULZ

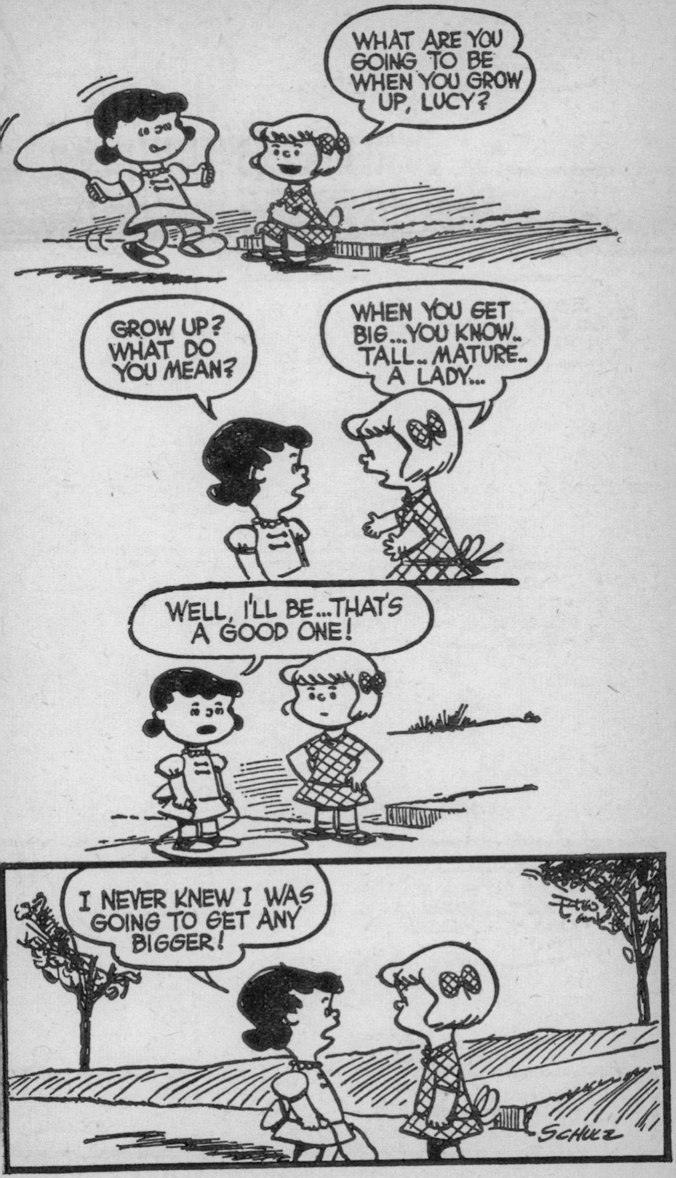
WHAT ARE YOU GOING TO BE WHEN YOU GROW UP, LUCY?
GROW UP? WHAT DO YOU MEAN?
WHEN YOU GET BIG...YOU KNOW.. TALL.. MATURE.. A LADY...
WELL, I'LL BE...THAT'S A GOOD ONE!
I NEVER KNEW I WAS GOING TO GET ANY BIGGER!
SCHULZ

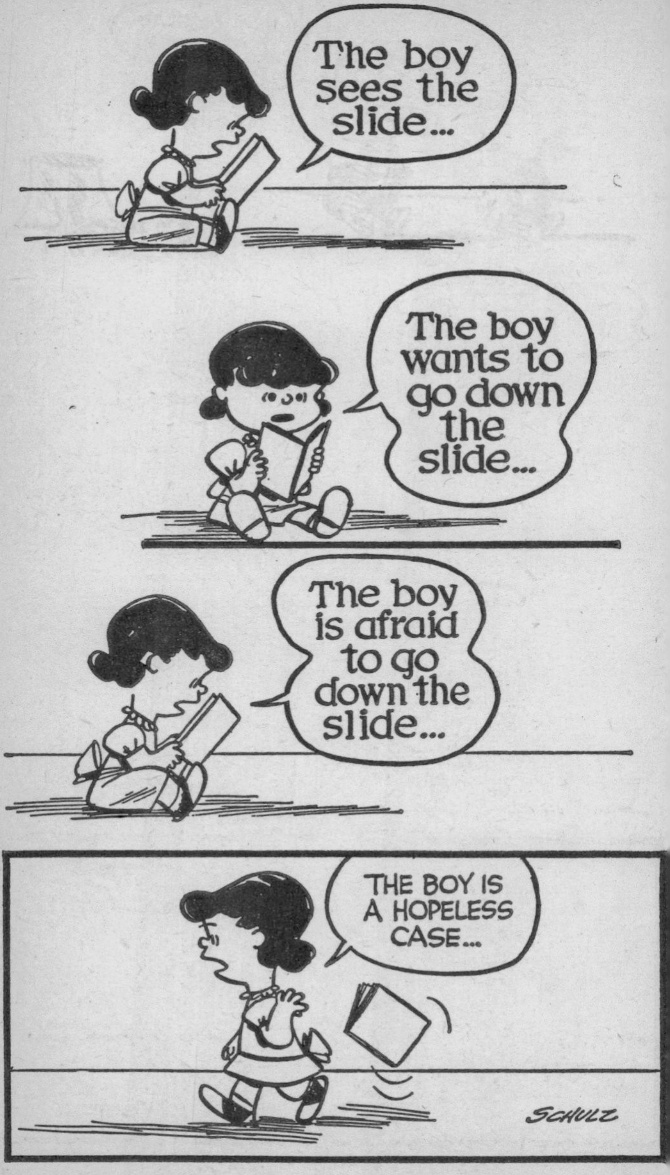
The boy sees the slide...
The boy wants to go down the slide...
The boy is afraid to go down the slide...
THE BOY IS A HOPELESS CASE...
SCHULZ

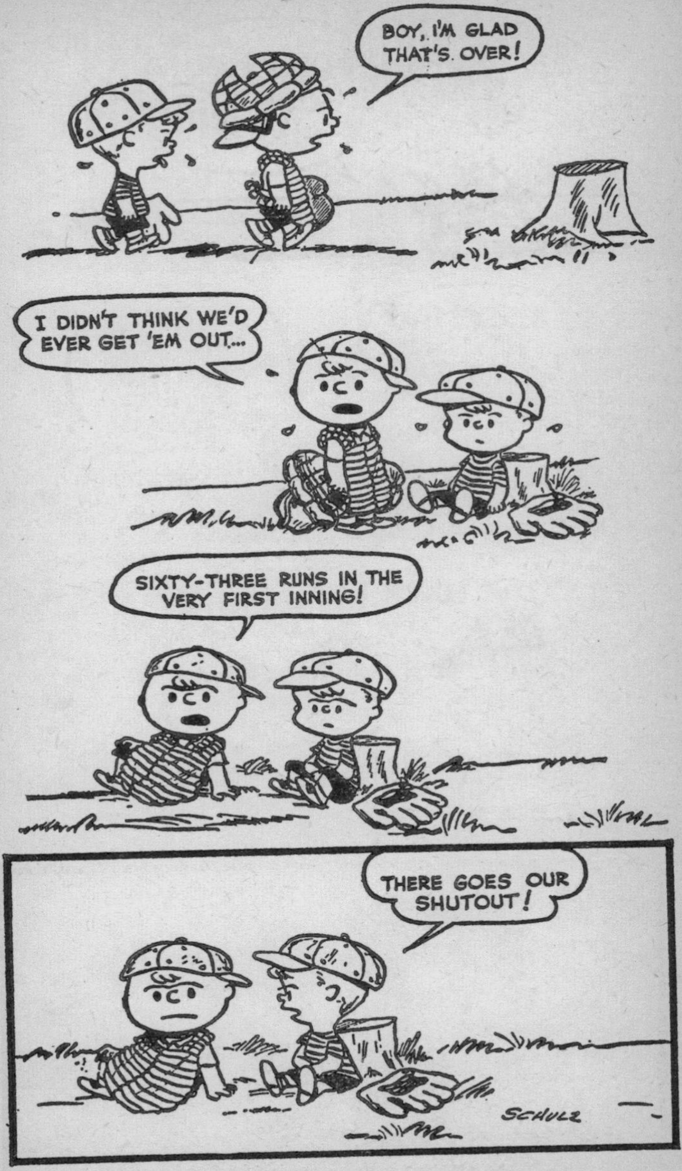
BOY, I'M GLAD THAT'S OVER!
I DIDN'T THINK WE'D EVER GET 'EM OUT....
SIXTY-THREE RUNS IN THE VERY FIRST INNING!
THERE GOES OUR SHUTOUT!
SCHULZ

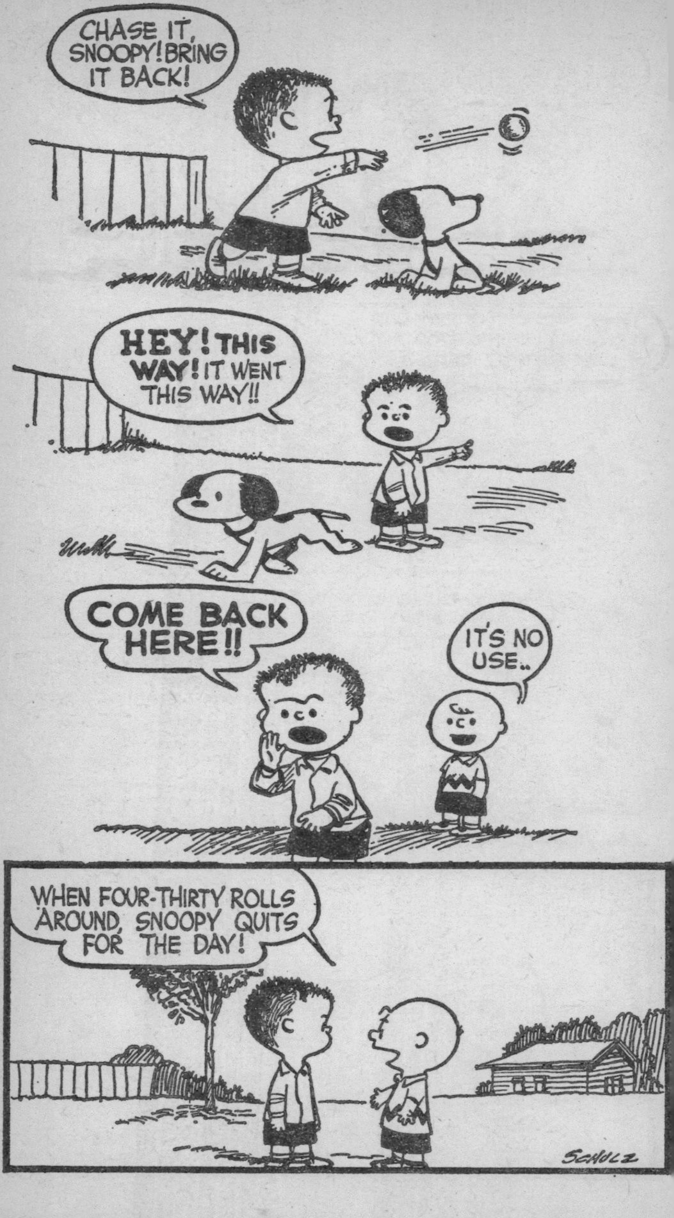
CHASE IT, SNOOPY! BRING IT BACK!
HEY! THIS WAY! IT WENT THIS WAY!!
COME BACK HERE!!
IT'S NO USE..
WHEN FOUR-THIRTY ROLLS AROUND, SNOOPY QUITS FOR THE DAY!
SCHULZ

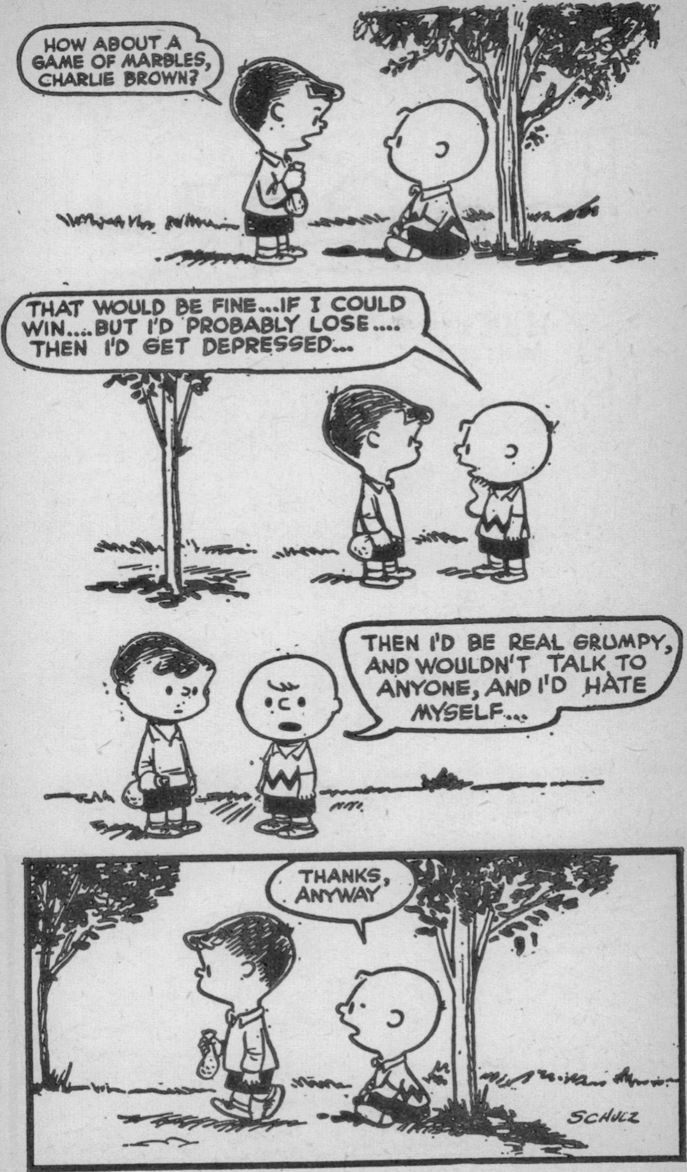
HOW ABOUT A GAME OF MARBLES, CHARLIE BROWN?
THAT WOULD BE FINE...IF I COULD WIN....BUT I'D PROBABLY LOSE.... THEN I'D GET DEPRESSED...
THEN I'D BE REAL GRUMPY, AND WOULDN'T TALK TO ANYONE, AND I'D HATE MYSELF...
THANKS, ANYWAY
SCHULZ

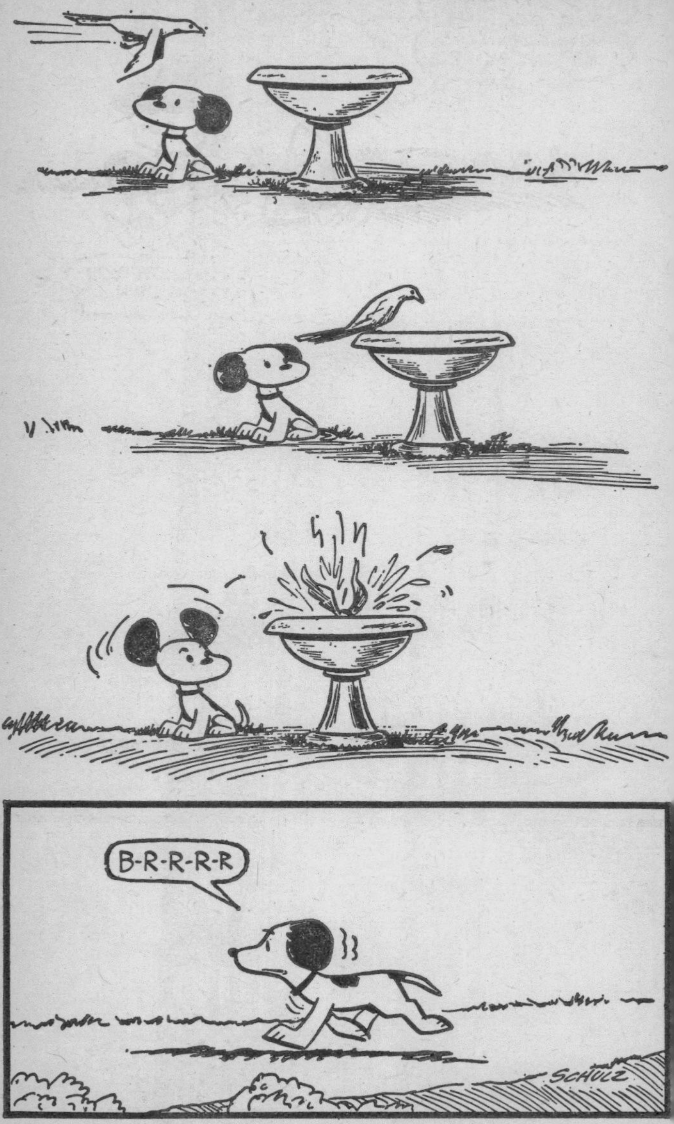
B-R-R-R-R
SCHULZ

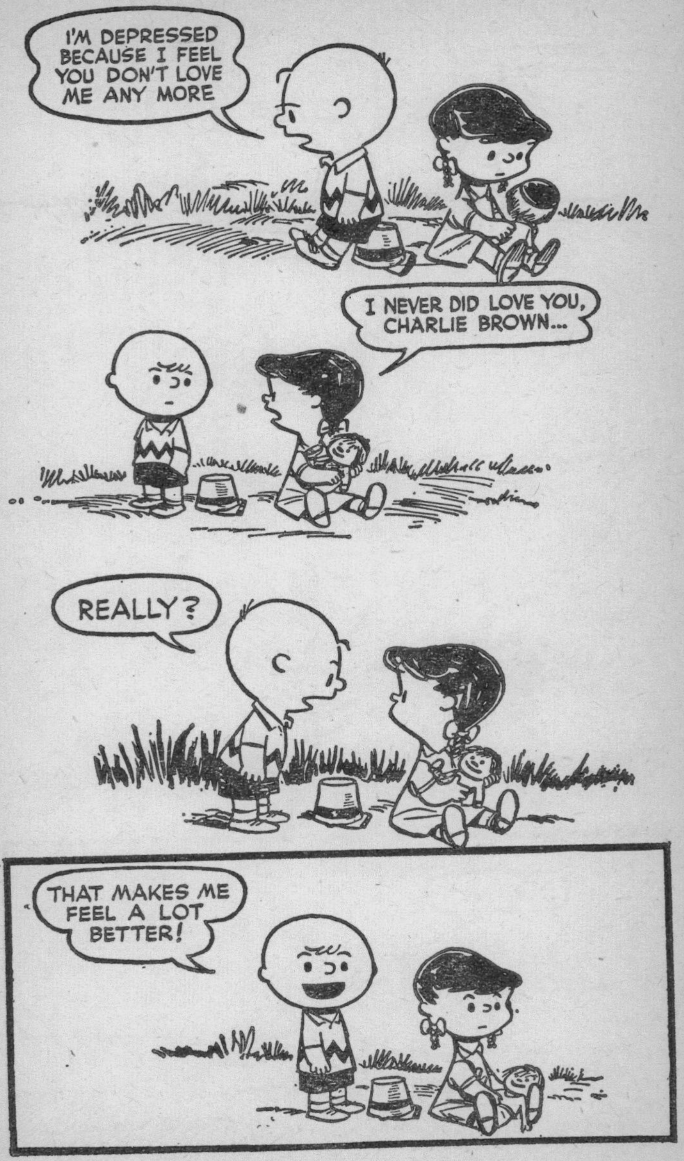
I'M DEPRESSED BECAUSE I FEEL YOU DON'T LOVE ME ANY MORE
I NEVER DID LOVE YOU, CHARLIE BROWN...
REALLY?
THAT MAKES ME FEEL A LOT BETTER!

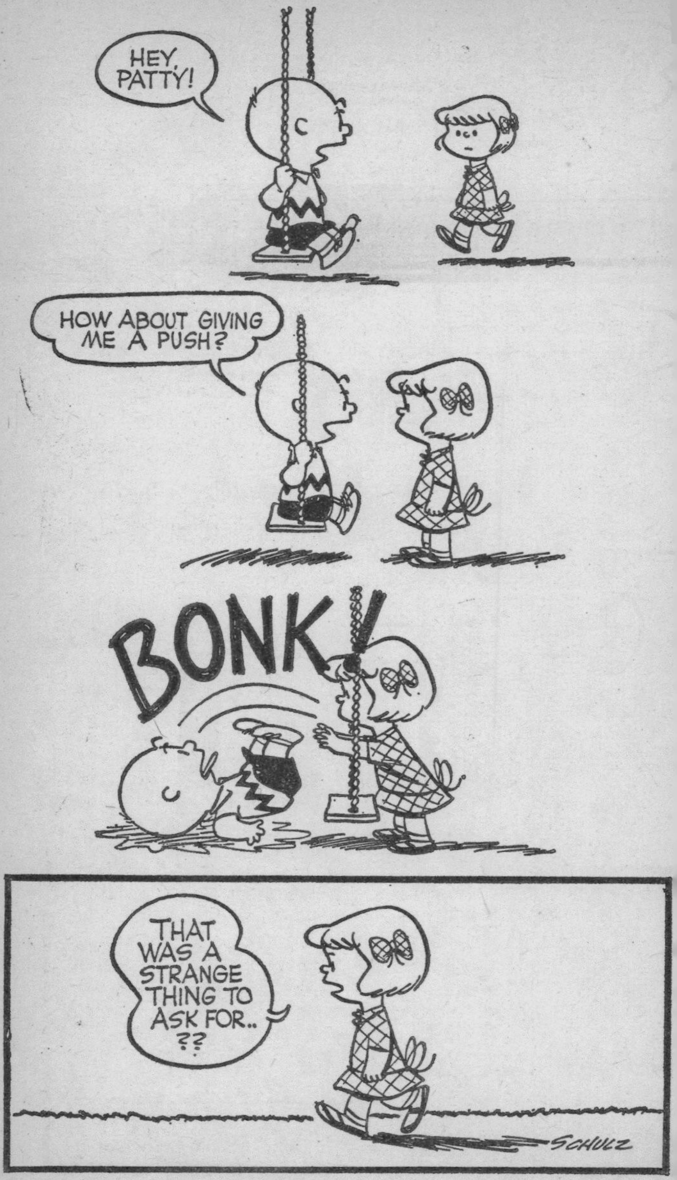
HEY, PATTY!
HOW ABOUT GIVING ME A PUSH?
BONK!
THAT WAS A STRANGE THING TO ASK FOR.. ??
SCHULZ

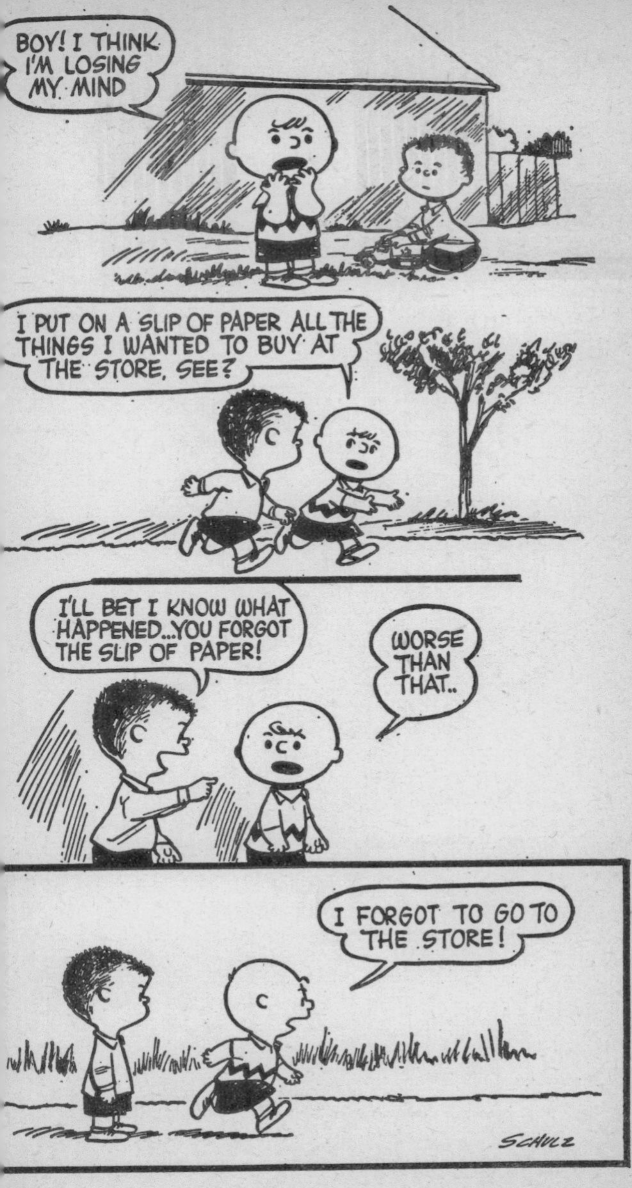
BOY! I THINK I'M LOSING MY MIND
I PUT ON A SLIP OF PAPER ALL THE THINGS I WANTED TO BUY AT THE STORE, SEE?
I'LL BET I KNOW WHAT HAPPENED...YOU FORGOT THE SLIP OF PAPER!
WORSE THAN THAT..
I FORGOT TO GO TO THE STORE!
SCHULZ

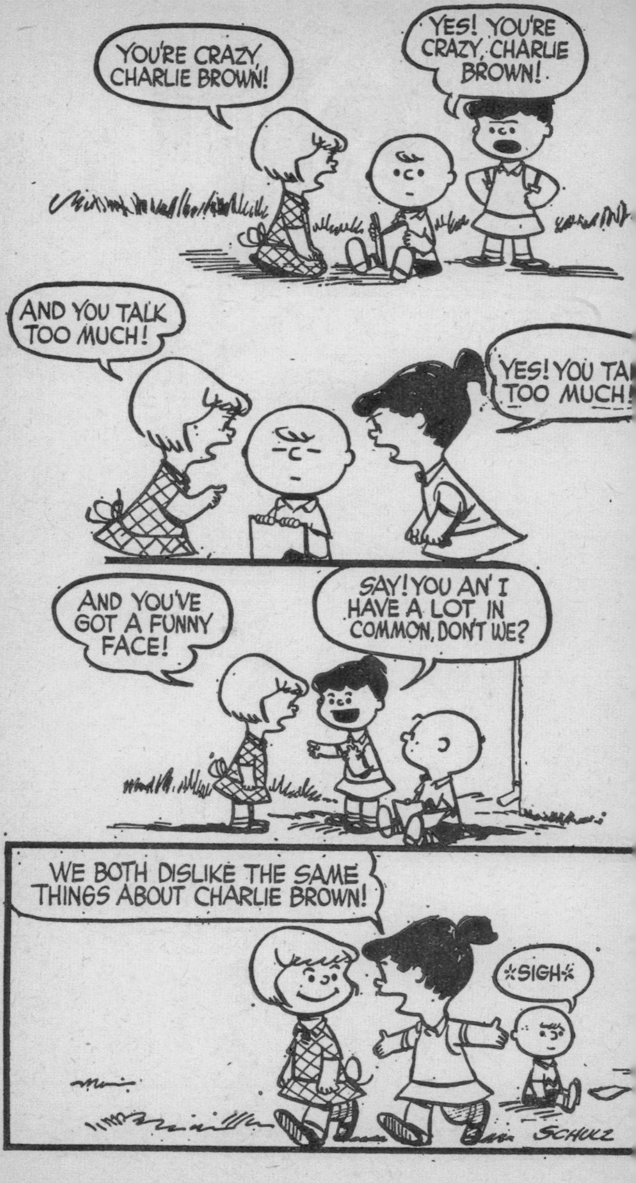
YOU'RE CRAZY, CHARLIE BROWN!
YES! YOU'RE CRAZY, CHARLIE BROWN!
AND YOU TALK TOO MUCH!
YES! YOU TA TOO MUCH!
AND YOU'VE GOT A FUNNY FACE!
SAY! YOU AN' I HAVE A LOT IN COMMON, DON'T WE?
WE BOTH DISLIKE THE SAME THINGS ABOUT CHARLIE BROWN!
SIGH
SCHULZ

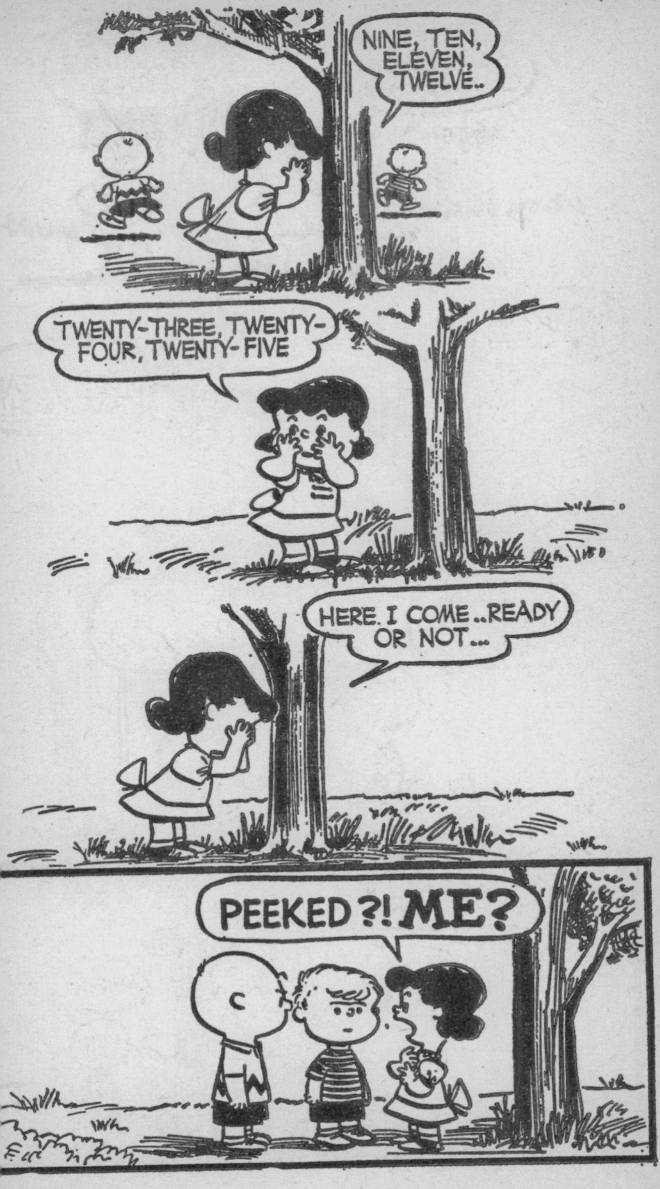

NINE, TEN, ELEVEN, TWELVE..
TWENTY-THREE, TWENTY-FOUR, TWENTY-FIVE
HERE. I COME..READY OR NOT...
PEEKED?! ME?

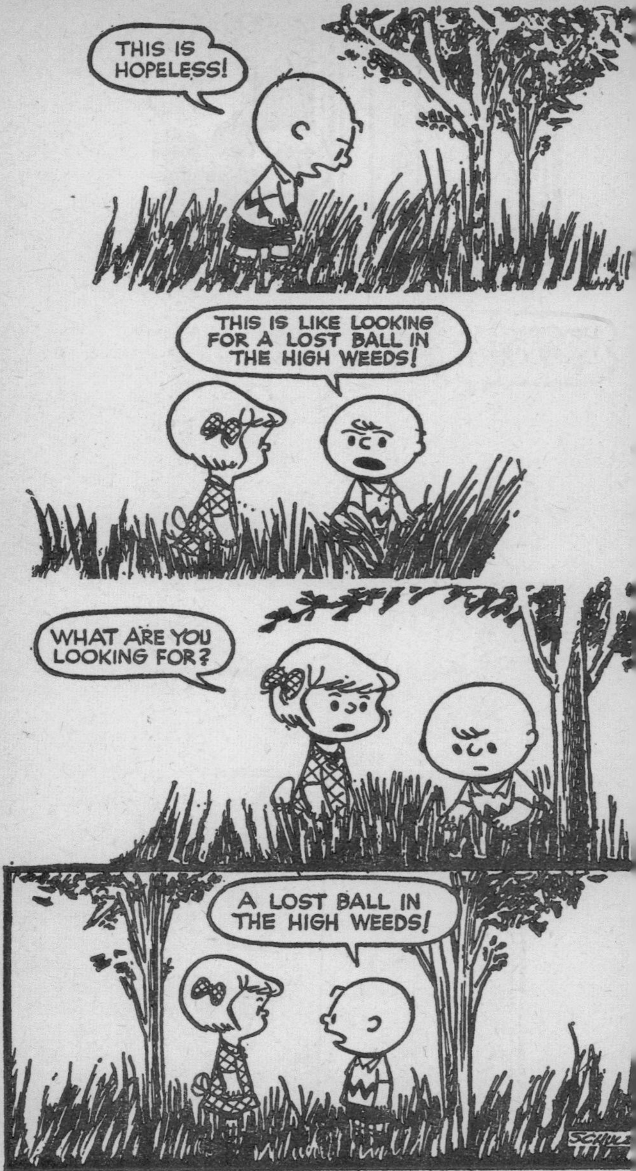
THIS IS HOPELESS!
THIS IS LIKE LOOKING FOR A LOST BALL IN THE HIGH WEEDS!
WHAT ARE YOU LOOKING FOR?
A LOST BALL IN THE HIGH WEEDS!
SCHULZ

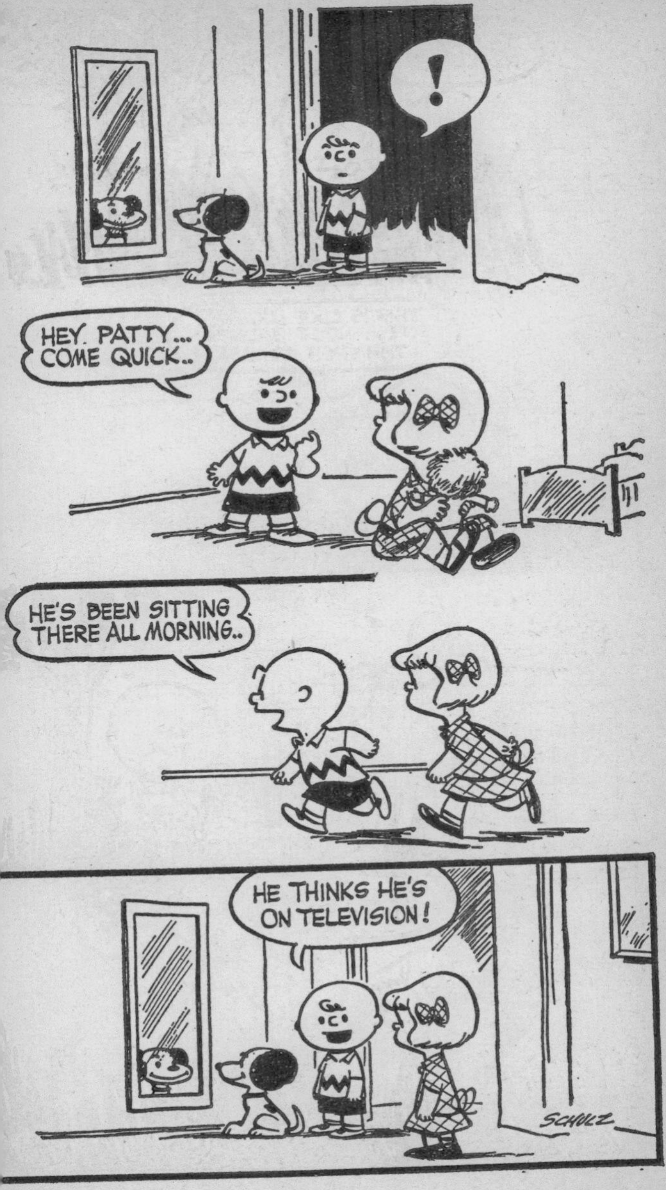
!
HEY PATTY... COME QUICK..
HE'S BEEN SITTING THERE ALL MORNING..
HE THINKS HE'S ON TELEVISION!
SCHULZ

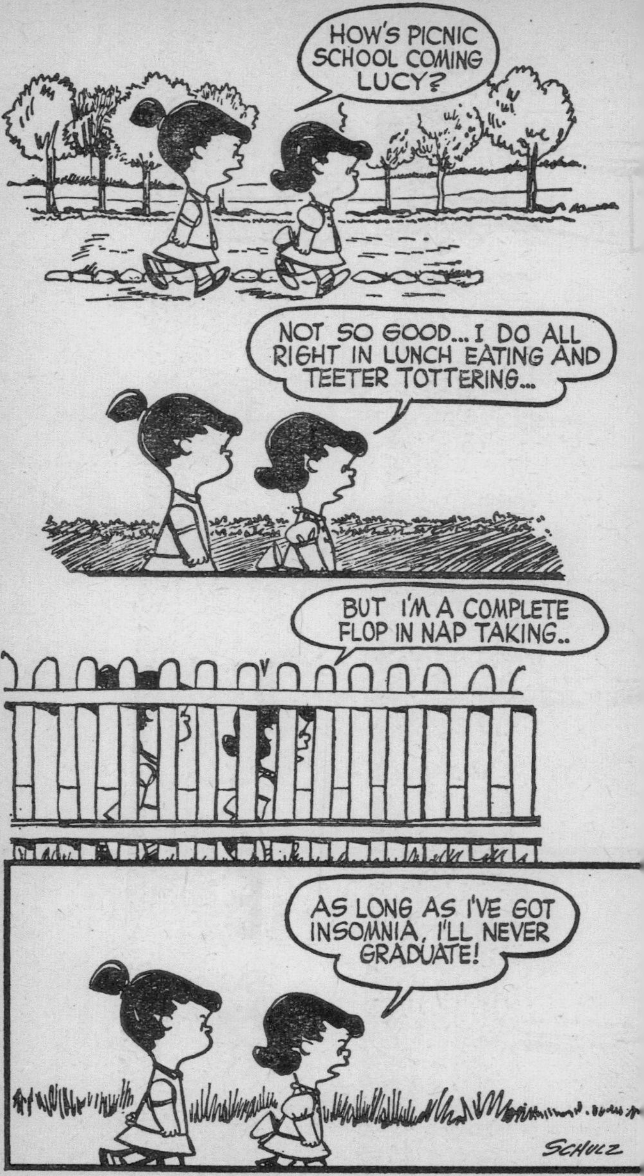
HOW'S PICNIC SCHOOL COMING LUCY?
NOT SO GOOD... I DO ALL RIGHT IN LUNCH EATING AND TEETER TOTTERING...
BUT I'M A COMPLETE FLOP IN NAP TAKING..
AS LONG AS I'VE GOT INSOMNIA, I'LL NEVER GRADUATE!
SCHULZ

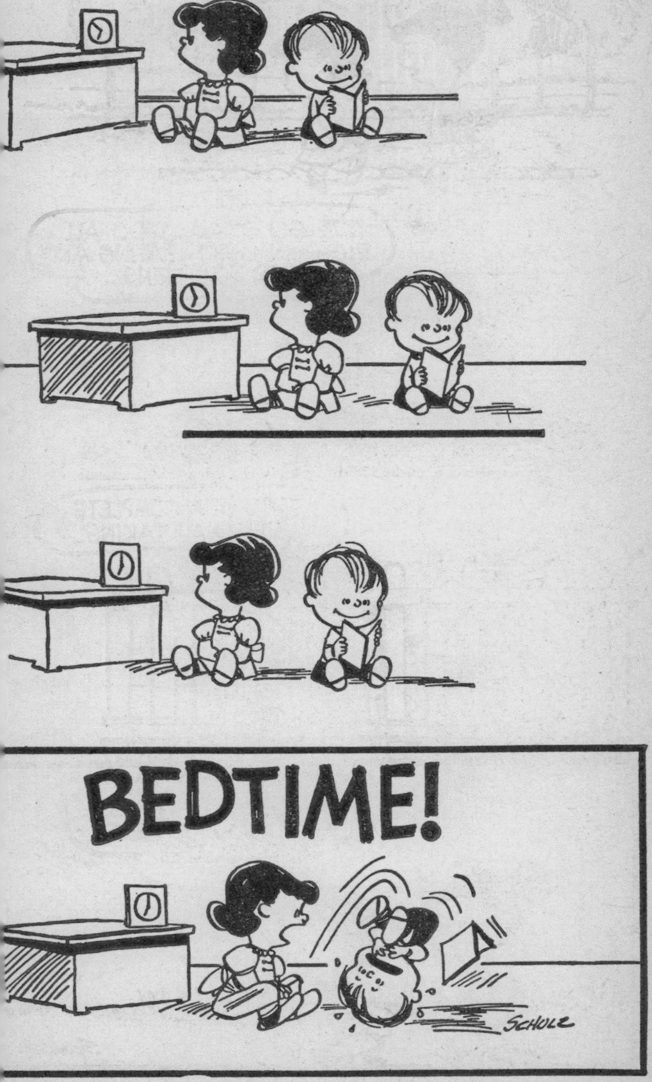
BEDTIME!
SCHULZ

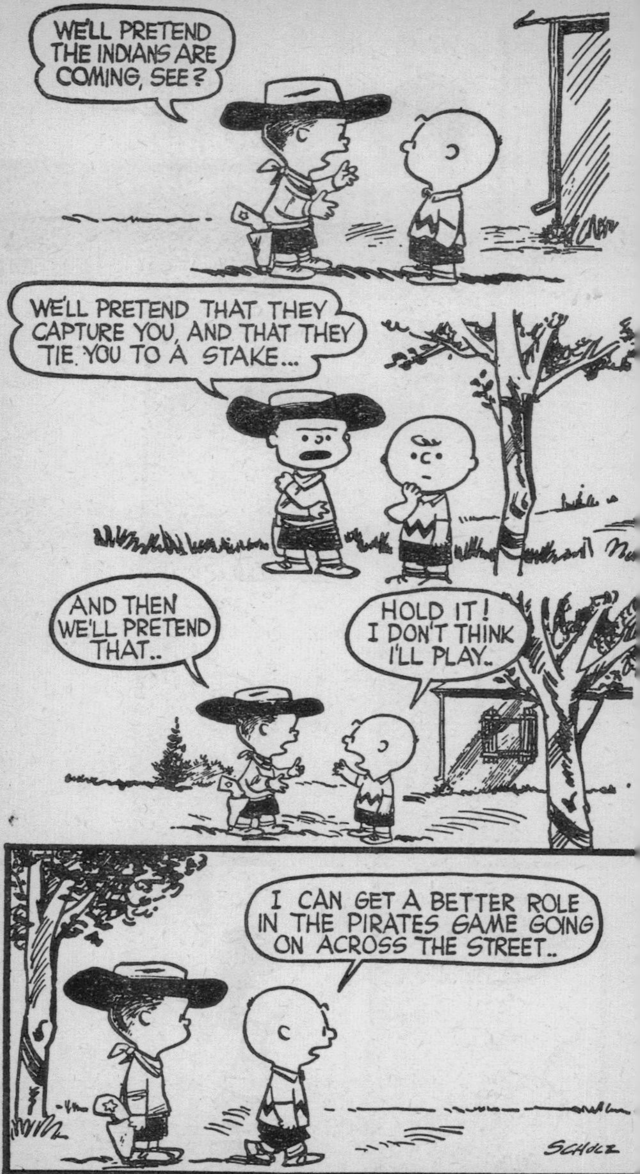
WE'LL PRETEND THE INDIANS ARE COMING, SEE?
WE'LL PRETEND THAT THEY CAPTURE YOU, AND THAT THEY TIE YOU TO A STAKE...
AND THEN WE'LL PRETEND THAT..
HOLD IT! I DON'T THINK I'LL PLAY..
I CAN GET A BETTER ROLE IN THE PIRATES GAME GOING ON ACROSS THE STREET..
SCHULZ

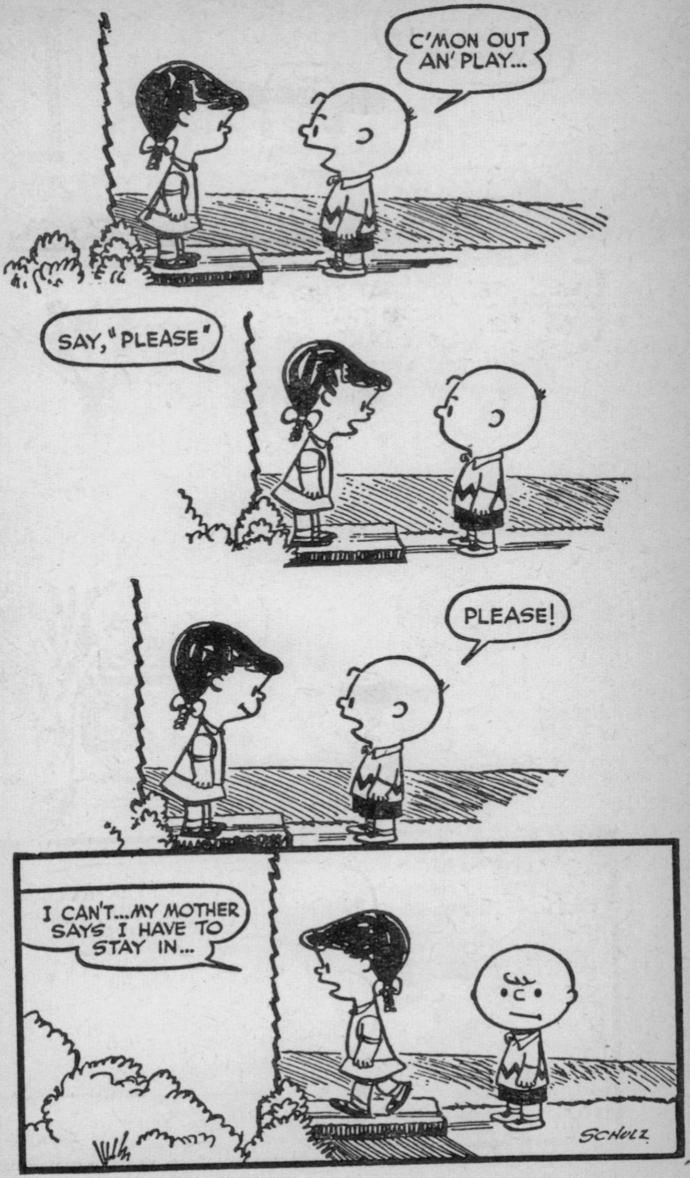
C'MON OUT AN' PLAY...
SAY, "PLEASE"
PLEASE!
I CAN'T...MY MOTHER SAYS I HAVE TO STAY IN...
SCHULZ

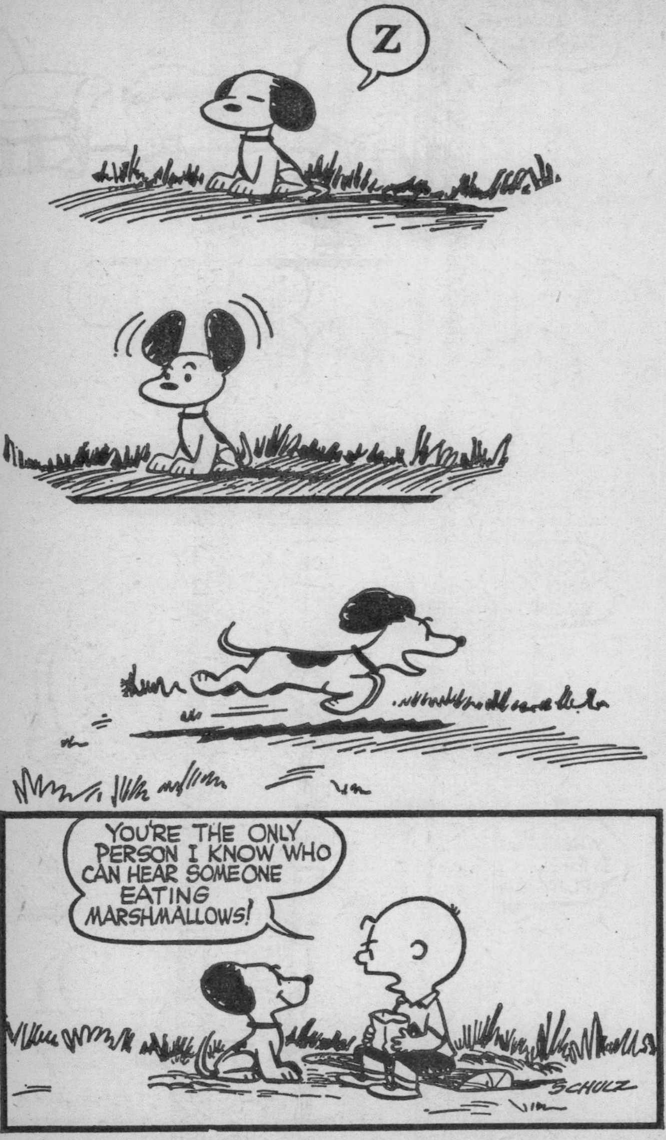
Z
YOU'RE THE ONLY PERSON I KNOW WHO CAN HEAR SOMEONE EATING MARSHMALLOWS!
SCHULZ

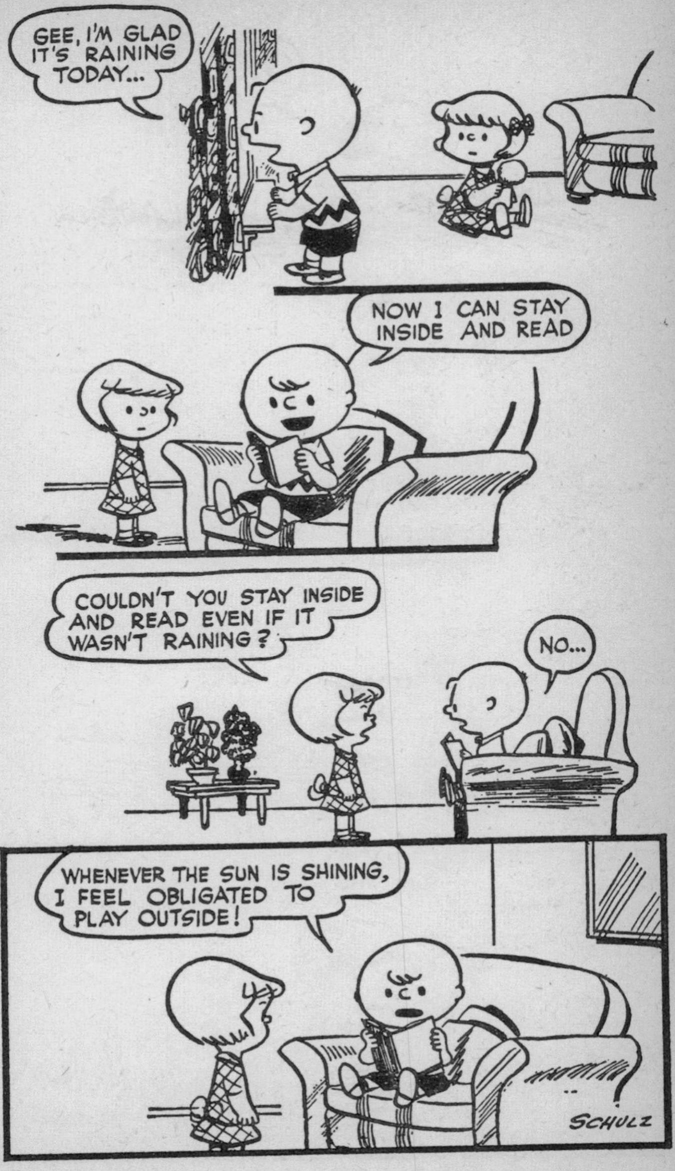
GEE, I'M GLAD IT'S RAINING TODAY...
NOW I CAN STAY INSIDE AND READ
COULDN'T YOU STAY INSIDE AND READ EVEN IF IT WASN'T RAINING?
NO...
WHENEVER THE SUN IS SHINING, I FEEL OBLIGATED TO PLAY OUTSIDE!
SCHULZ

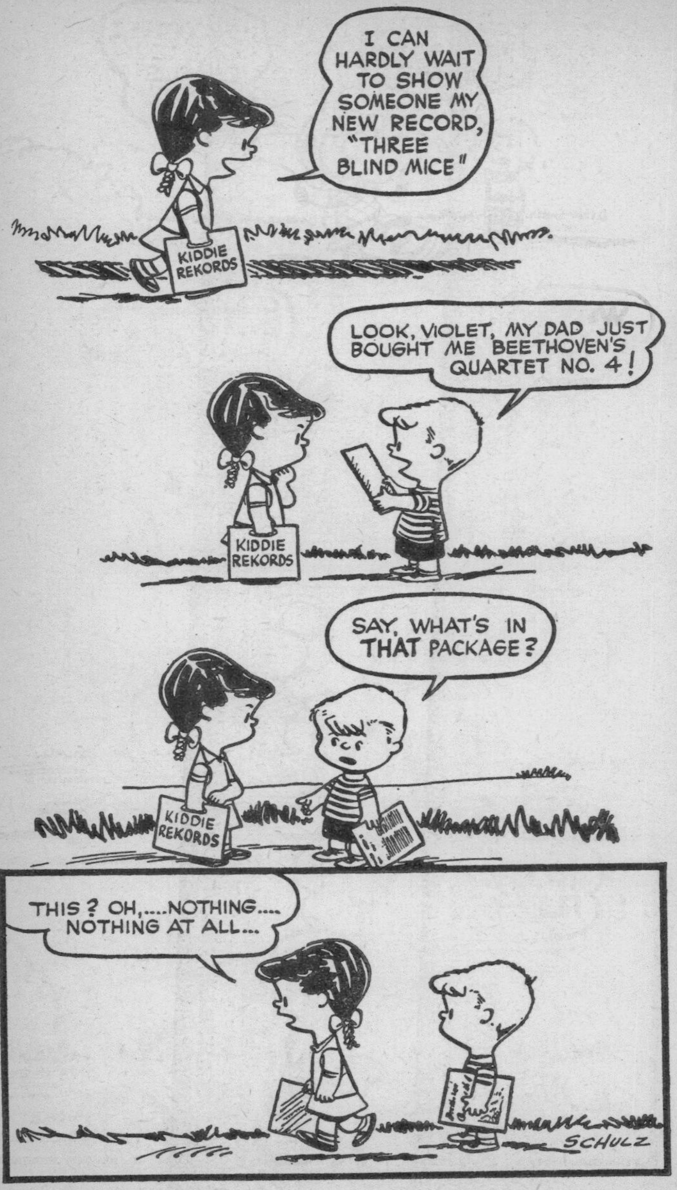
I CAN HARDLY WAIT TO SHOW SOMEONE MY NEW RECORD, "THREE BLIND MICE"
KIDDIE REKORDS
LOOK, VIOLET, MY DAD JUST BOUGHT ME BEETHOVEN'S QUARTET NO. 4!
KIDDIE REKORDS
SAY, WHAT'S IN THAT PACKAGE?
KIDDIE REKORDS
THIS? OH,....NOTHING.... NOTHING AT ALL...
SCHULZ

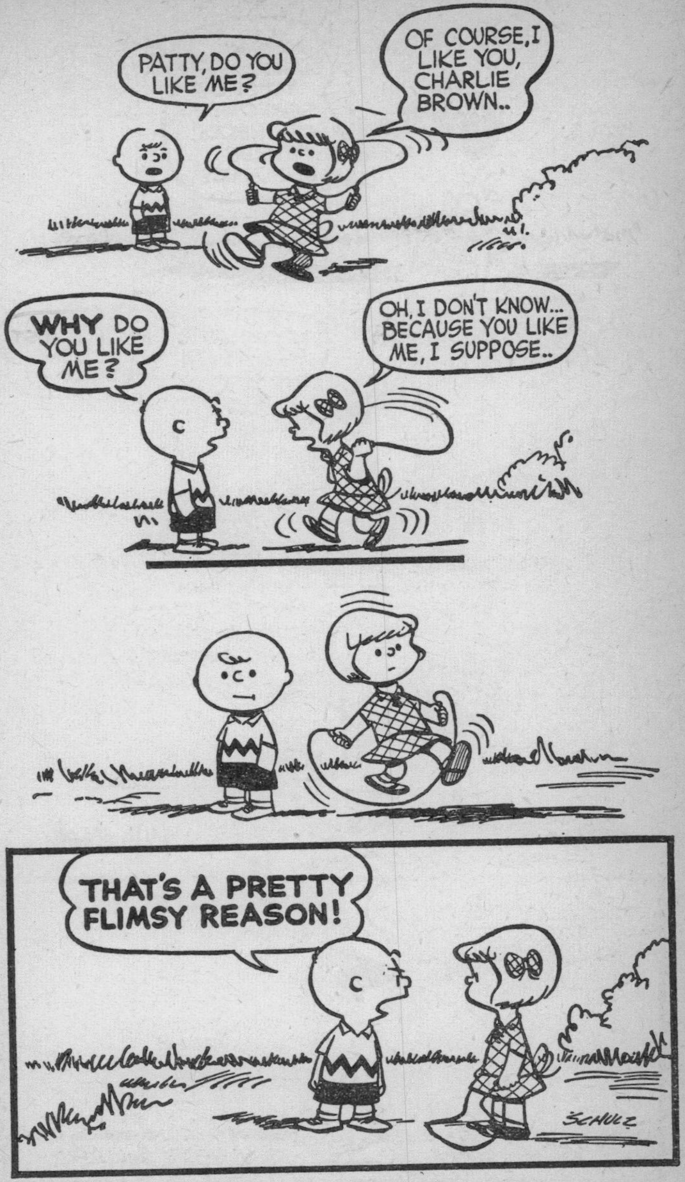
PATTY, DO YOU LIKE ME?
OF COURSE, I LIKE YOU, CHARLIE BROWN..
WHY DO YOU LIKE ME?
OH, I DON'T KNOW... BECAUSE YOU LIKE ME, I SUPPOSE..
THAT'S A PRETTY FLIMSY REASON!
SCHULZ

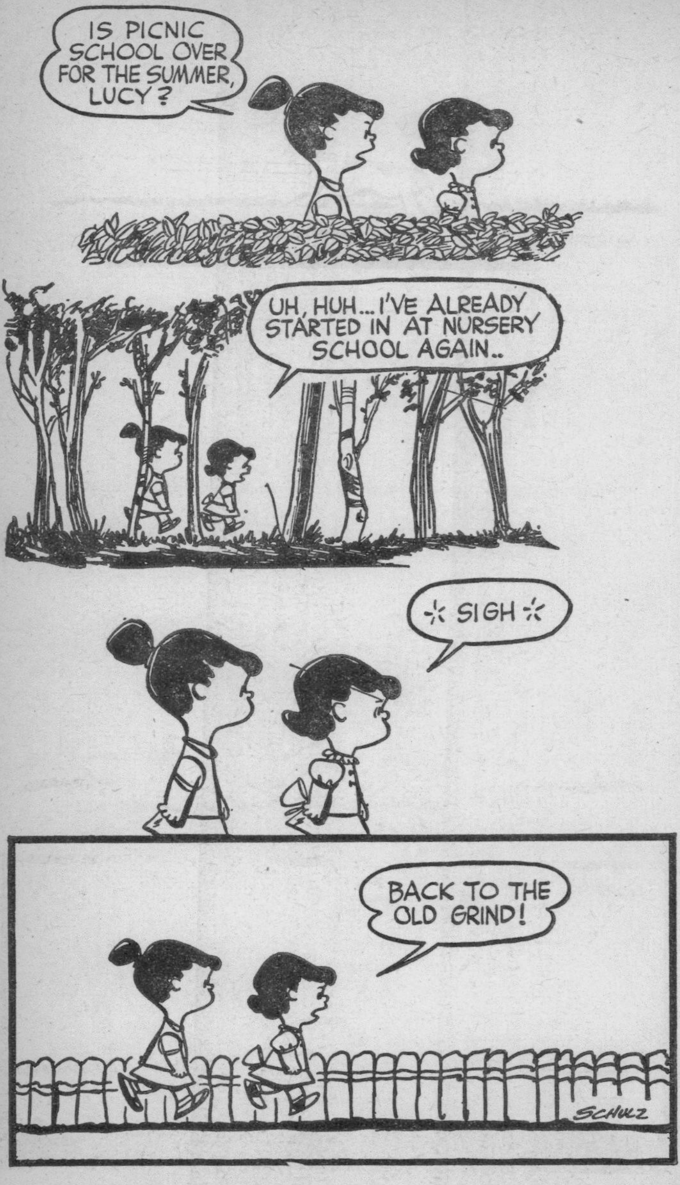
IS PICNIC SCHOOL OVER FOR THE SUMMER, LUCY?
UH, HUH... I'VE ALREADY STARTED IN AT NURSERY SCHOOL AGAIN..
SIGH
BACK TO THE OLD GRIND!
SCHULZ

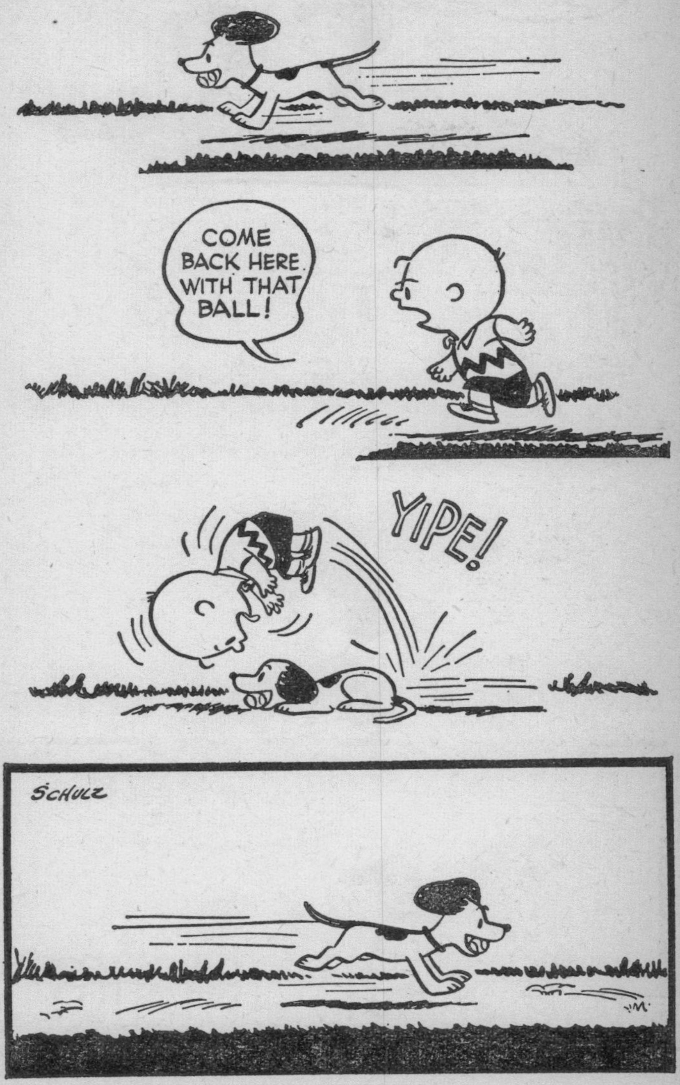
COME BACK HERE WITH THAT BALL!
YIPE!
SCHULZ

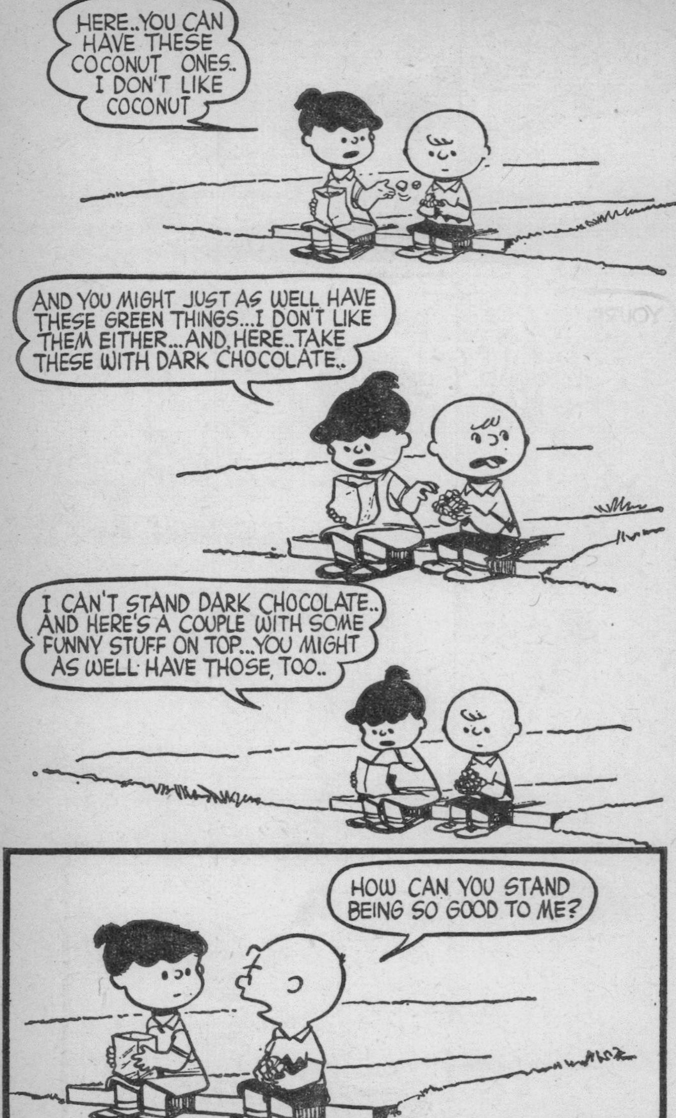
HERE..YOU CAN HAVE THESE COCONUT ONES.. I DON'T LIKE COCONUT
AND YOU MIGHT JUST AS WELL HAVE THESE GREEN THINGS...I DON'T LIKE THEM EITHER...AND, HERE..TAKE THESE WITH DARK CHOCOLATE..
I CAN'T STAND DARK CHOCOLATE.. AND HERE'S A COUPLE WITH SOME FUNNY STUFF ON TOP...YOU MIGHT AS WELL HAVE THOSE, TOO..
HOW CAN YOU STAND BEING SO GOOD TO ME?
SCHULZ

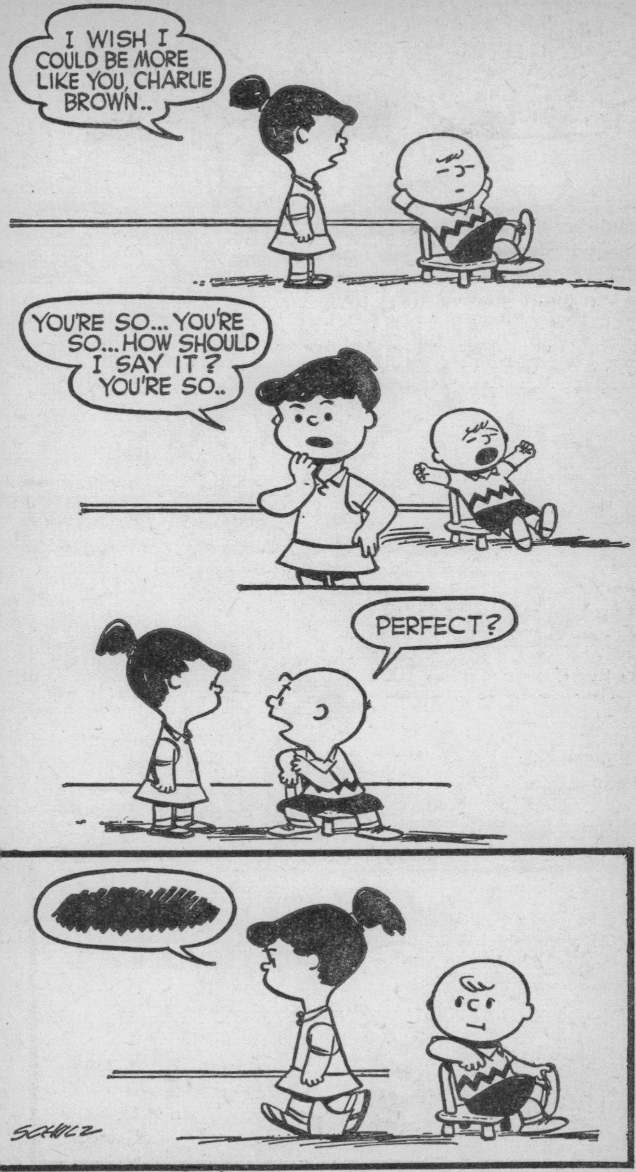
I WISH I COULD BE MORE LIKE YOU, CHARLIE BROWN..
YOU'RE SO... YOU'RE SO... HOW SHOULD I SAY IT? YOU'RE SO..
PERFECT?
SCHULZ

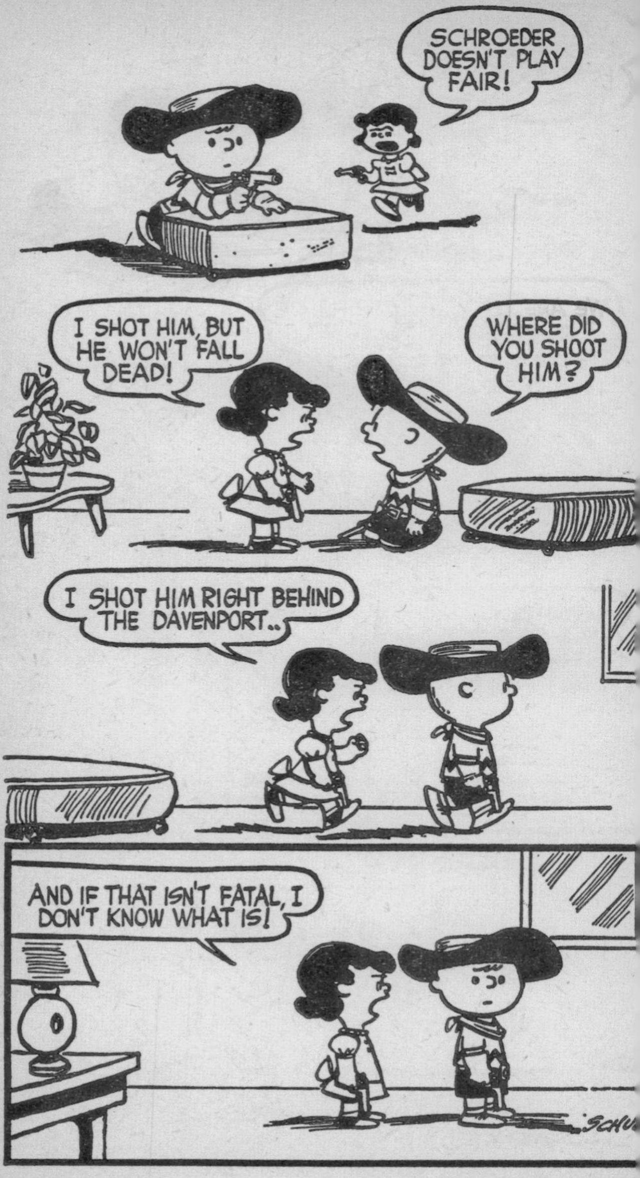
SCHROEDER DOESN'T PLAY FAIR!
I SHOT HIM, BUT HE WON'T FALL DEAD!
WHERE DID YOU SHOOT HIM?
I SHOT HIM RIGHT BEHIND THE DAVENPORT..
AND IF THAT ISN'T FATAL, I DON'T KNOW WHAT IS!

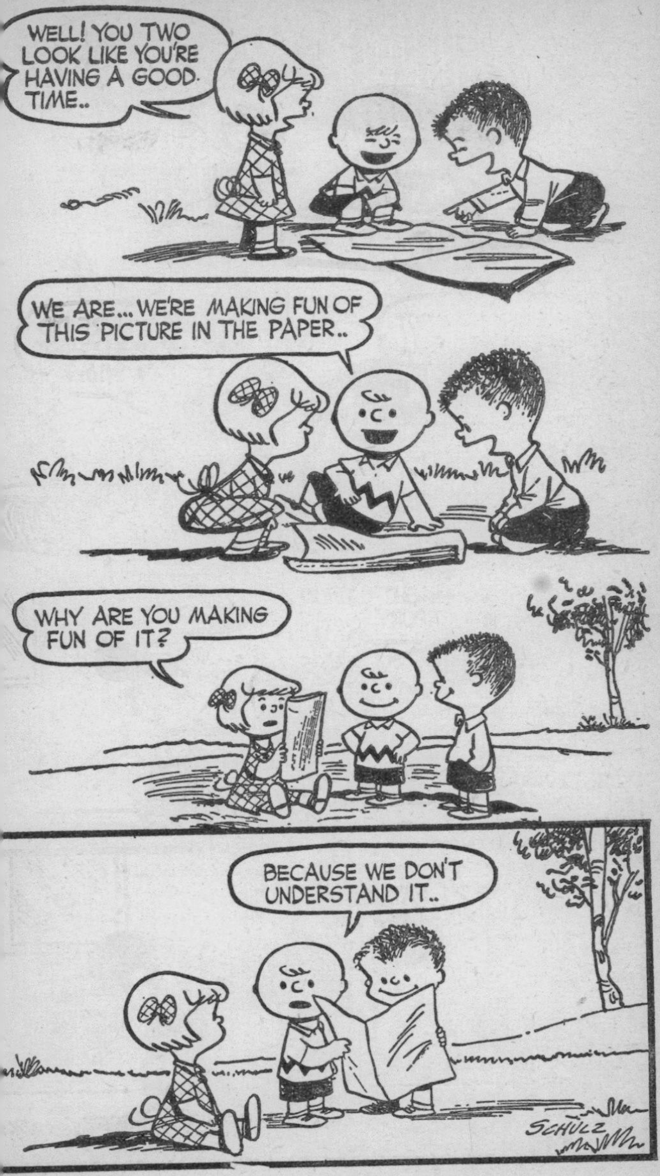
WELL! YOU TWO LOOK LIKE YOU'RE HAVING A GOOD TIME..
WE ARE... WE'RE MAKING FUN OF THIS PICTURE IN THE PAPER..
WHY ARE YOU MAKING FUN OF IT?
BECAUSE WE DON'T UNDERSTAND IT..
SCHULZ

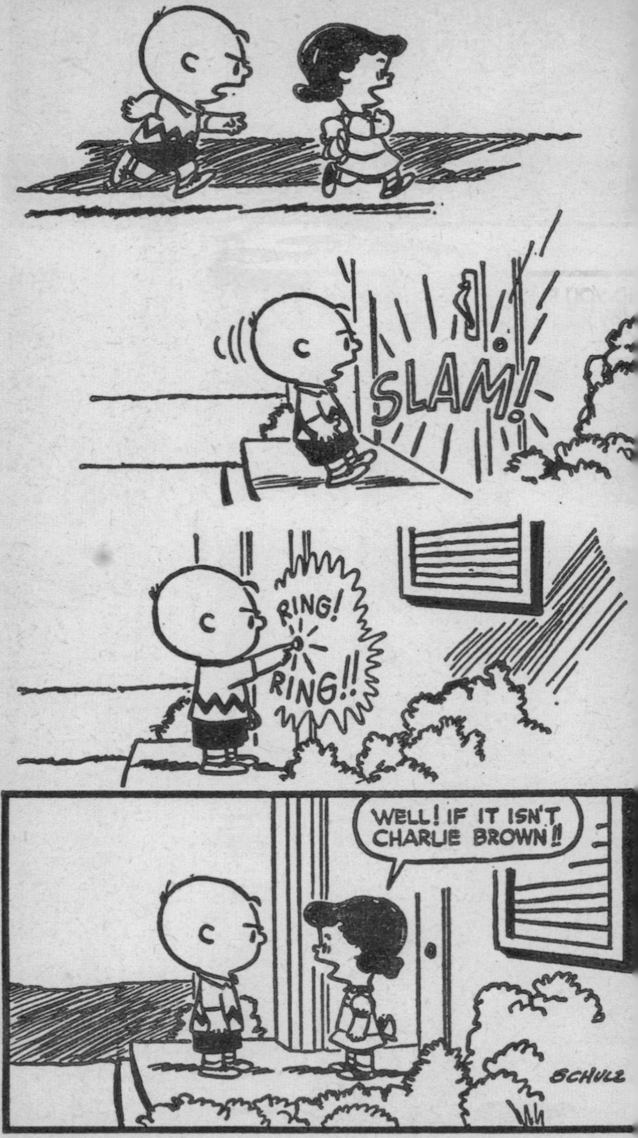
SLAM!
RING!
RING!!
WELL! IF IT ISN'T CHARLIE BROWN!!
SCHULZ

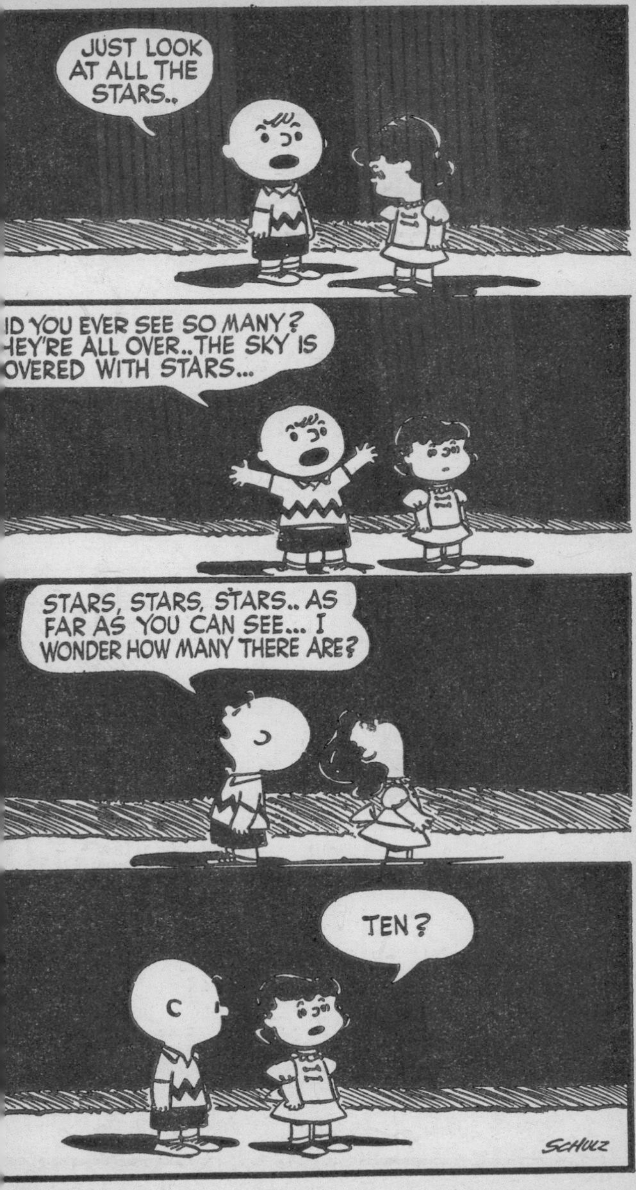
JUST LOOK AT ALL THE STARS..
ID YOU EVER SEE SO MANY? HEY'RE ALL OVER..THE SKY IS OVERED WITH STARS...
STARS, STARS, STARS.. AS FAR AS YOU CAN SEE... I WONDER HOW MANY THERE ARE?
TEN?
SCHULZ

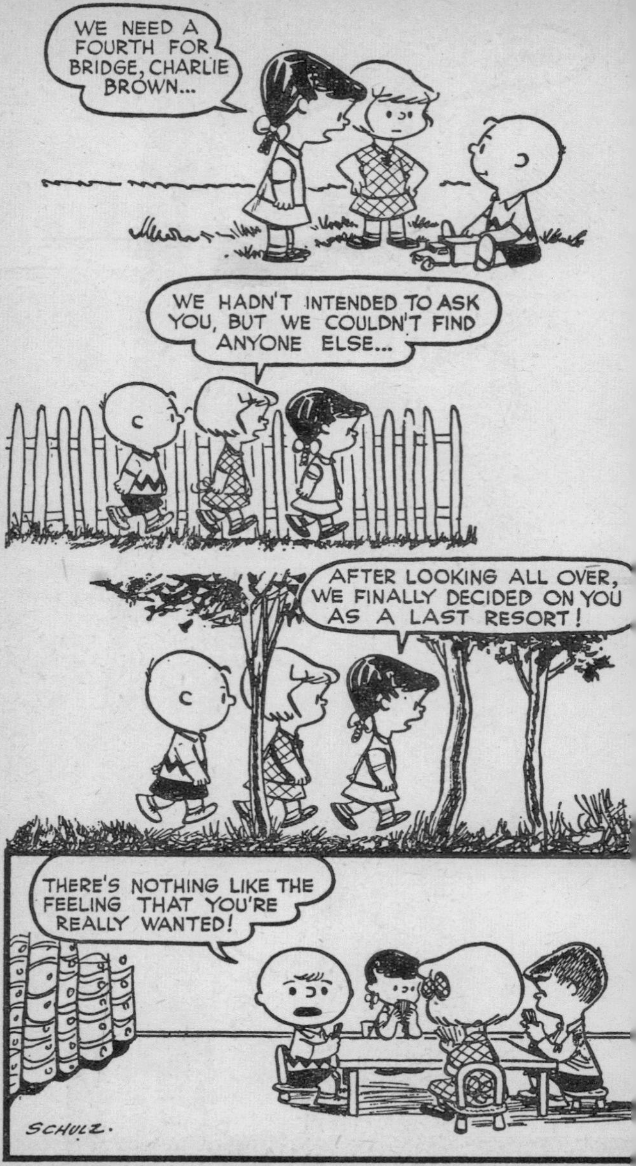
WE NEED A FOURTH FOR BRIDGE, CHARLIE BROWN...
WE HADN'T INTENDED TO ASK YOU, BUT WE COULDN'T FIND ANYONE ELSE...
AFTER LOOKING ALL OVER, WE FINALLY DECIDED ON YOU AS A LAST RESORT!
THERE'S NOTHING LIKE THE FEELING THAT YOU'RE REALLY WANTED!
SCHULZ.

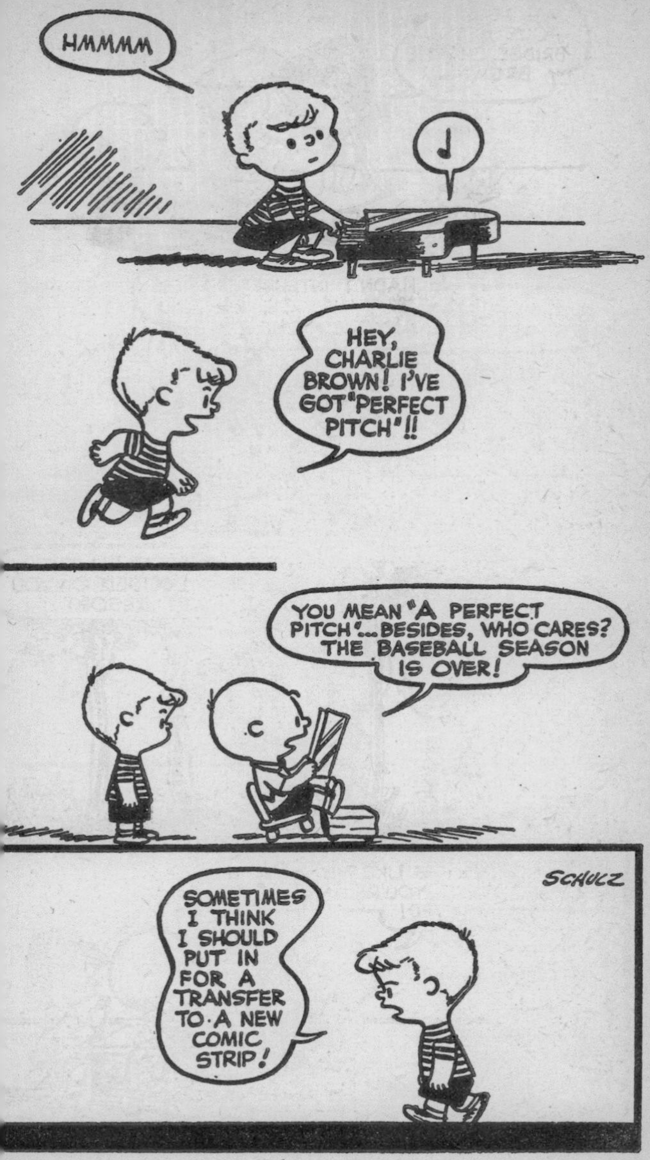
HMMMM
HEY, CHARLIE BROWN! I'VE GOT "PERFECT PITCH"!!
YOU MEAN "A PERFECT PITCH"... BESIDES, WHO CARES? THE BASEBALL SEASON IS OVER!
SCHULZ
SOMETIMES I THINK I SHOULD PUT IN FOR A TRANSFER TO A NEW COMIC STRIP!

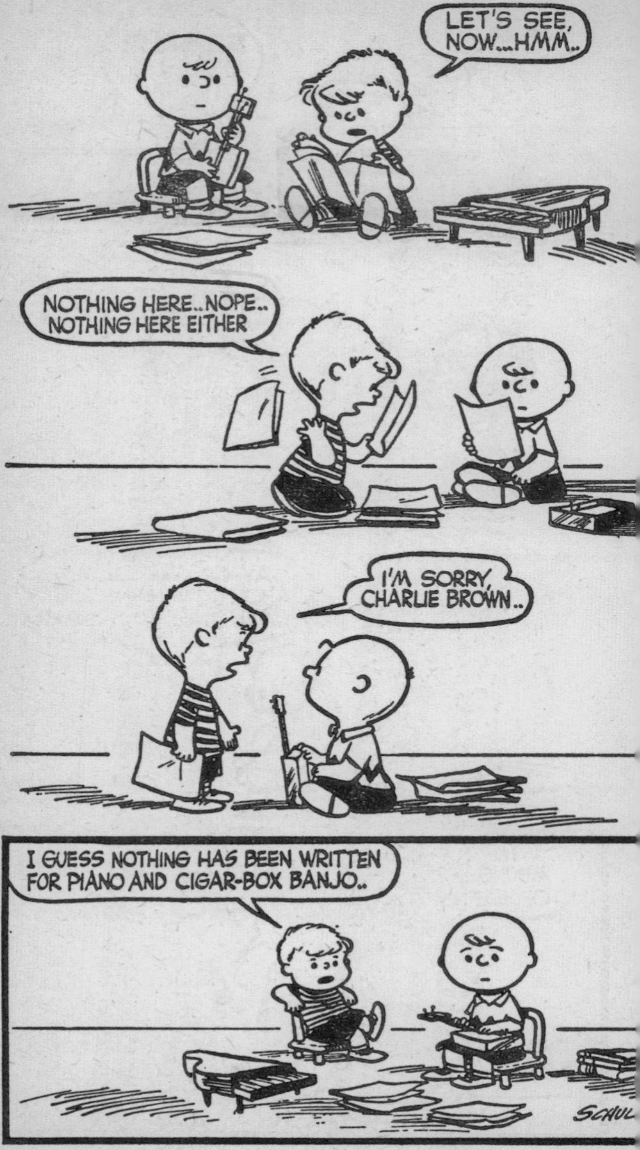
LET'S SEE, NOW...HMM..
NOTHING HERE..NOPE.. NOTHING HERE EITHER
I'M SORRY, CHARLIE BROWN..
I GUESS NOTHING HAS BEEN WRITTEN FOR PIANO AND CIGAR-BOX BANJO..
SCHUL

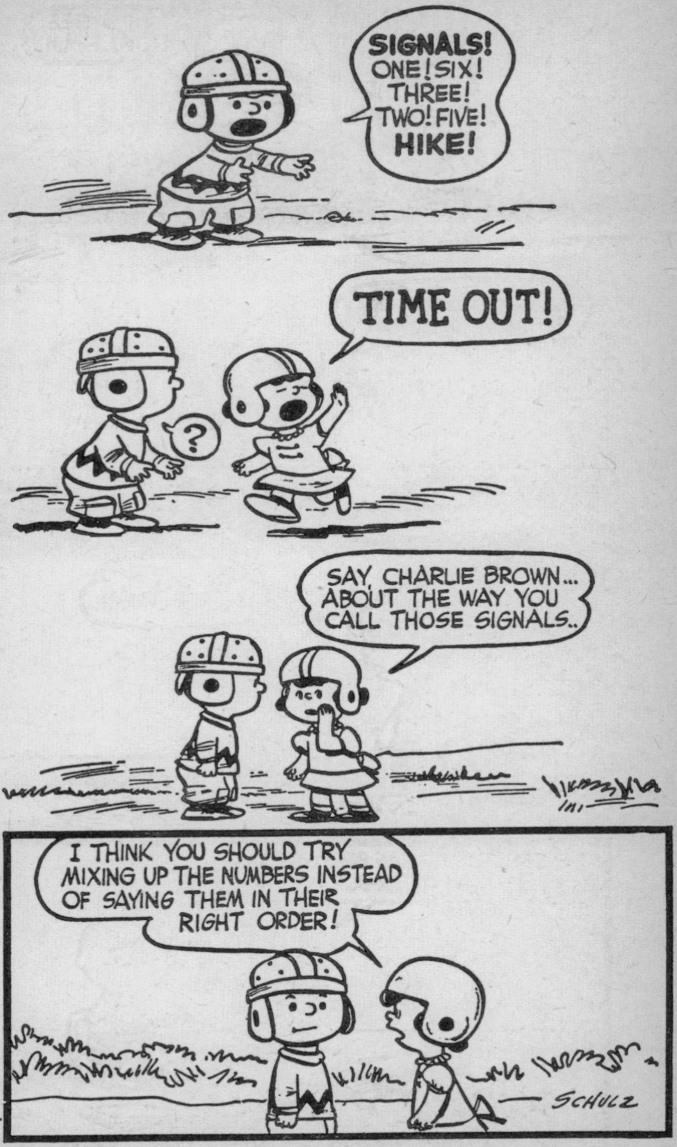
SIGNALS! ONE! SIX! THREE! TWO! FIVE! HIKE!
TIME OUT!
?
SAY, CHARLIE BROWN... ABOUT THE WAY YOU CALL THOSE SIGNALS..
I THINK YOU SHOULD TRY MIXING UP THE NUMBERS INSTEAD OF SAYING THEM IN THEIR RIGHT ORDER!
SCHULZ

BOY, AM I EVER DEPRESSED
SOMEBODY ELSE IS DEPRESSED TOO, I SEE
THAT'S THE ONLY THING THAT COULD POSSIBLY HAVE CHEERED ME UP!
SCHULZ

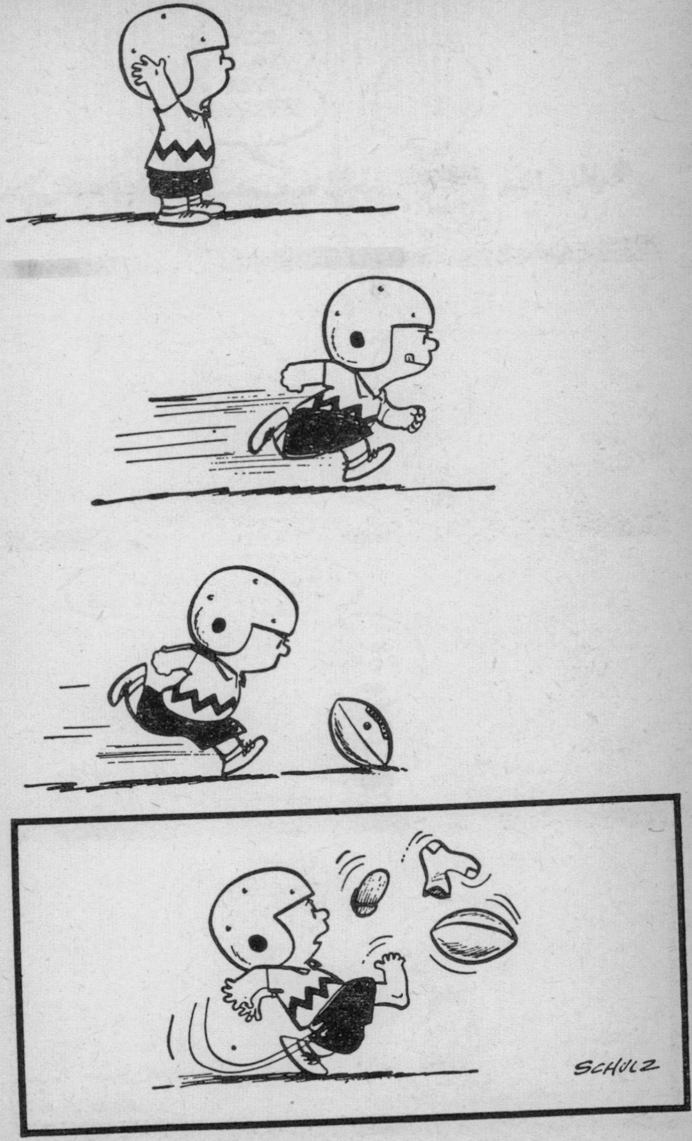
SCHULZ

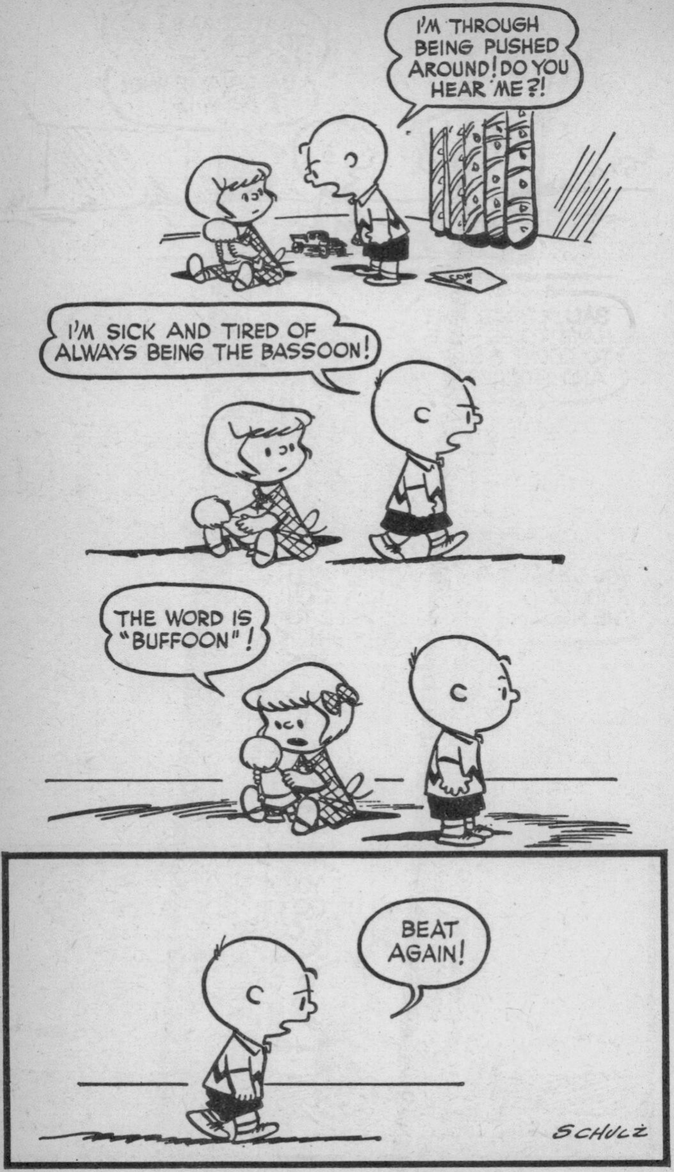
I'M THROUGH BEING PUSHED AROUND! DO YOU HEAR ME?!
I'M SICK AND TIRED OF ALWAYS BEING THE BASSOON!
THE WORD IS "BUFFOON"!
BEAT AGAIN!
SCHULZ

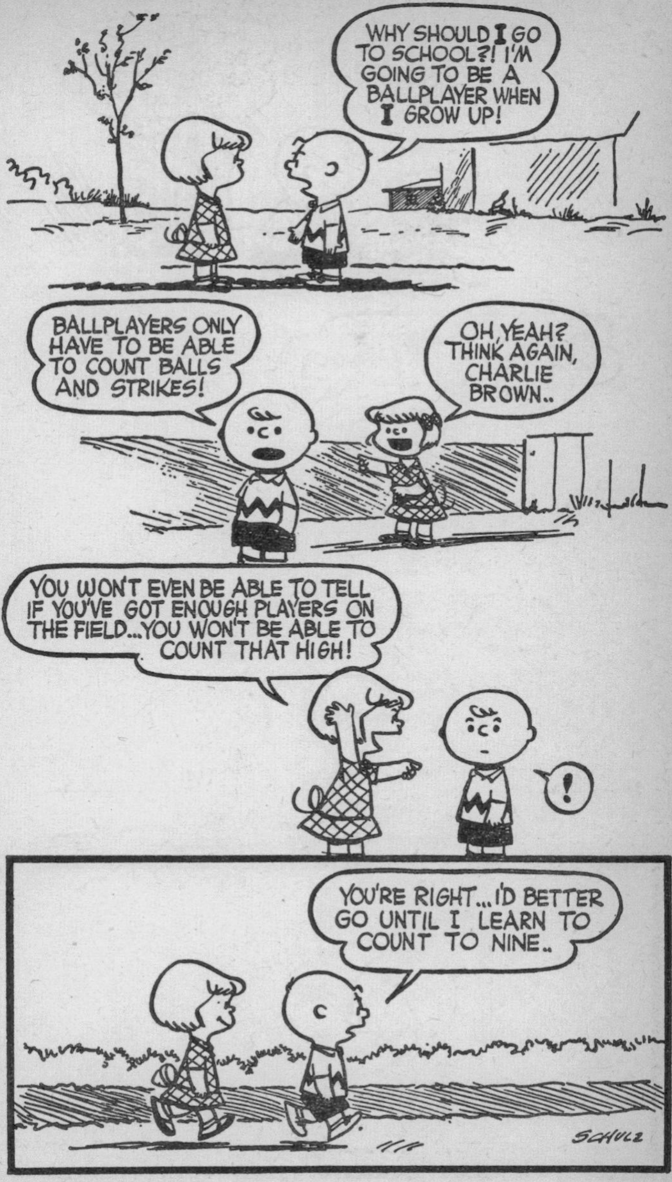
WHY SHOULD I GO TO SCHOOL?! I'M GOING TO BE A BALLPLAYER WHEN I GROW UP!
BALLPLAYERS ONLY HAVE TO BE ABLE TO COUNT BALLS AND STRIKES!
OH, YEAH? THINK AGAIN, CHARLIE BROWN..
YOU WON'T EVEN BE ABLE TO TELL IF YOU'VE GOT ENOUGH PLAYERS ON THE FIELD...YOU WON'T BE ABLE TO COUNT THAT HIGH!
!
YOU'RE RIGHT...I'D BETTER GO UNTIL I LEARN TO COUNT TO NINE..
SCHULZ

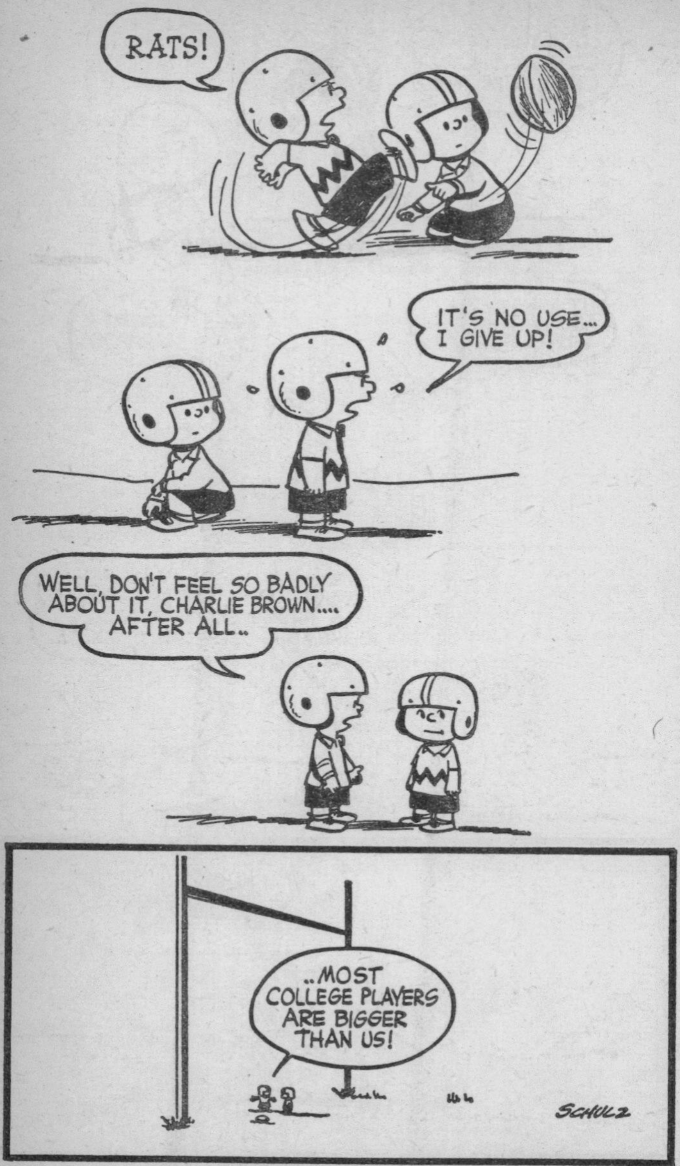
RATS!
IT'S NO USE... I GIVE UP!
WELL, DON'T FEEL SO BADLY ABOUT IT, CHARLIE BROWN.... AFTER ALL..
..MOST COLLEGE PLAYERS ARE BIGGER THAN US!
SCHULZ

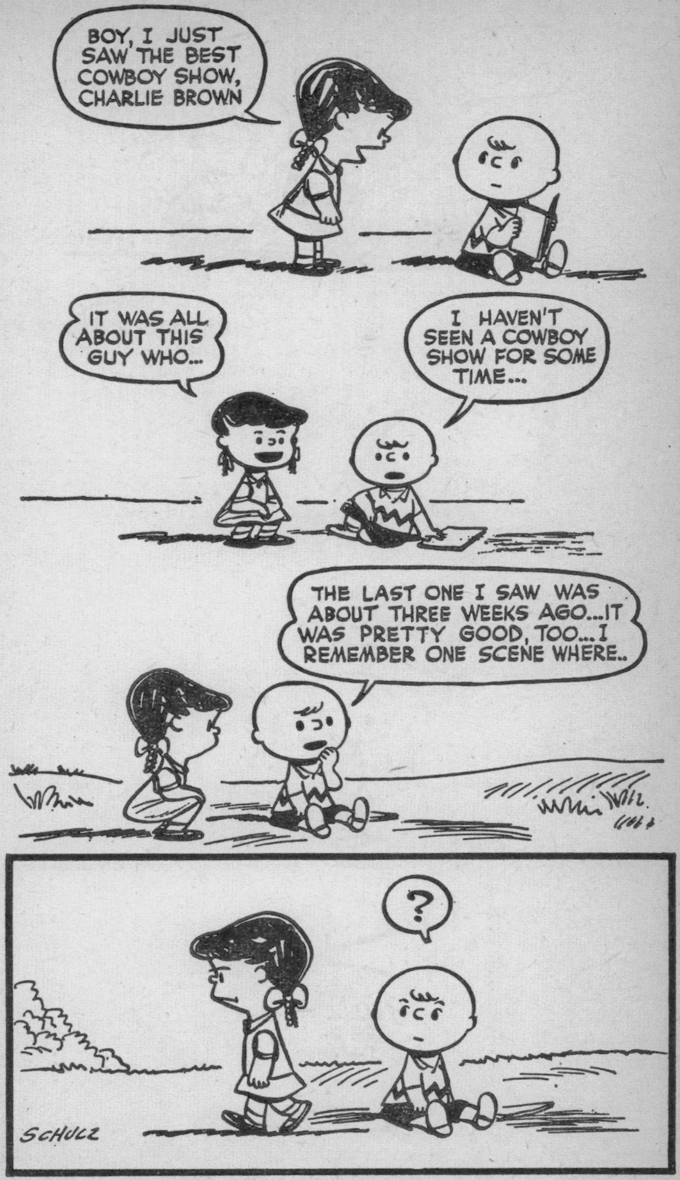
BOY, I JUST SAW THE BEST COWBOY SHOW, CHARLIE BROWN
IT WAS ALL ABOUT THIS GUY WHO...
I HAVEN'T SEEN A COWBOY SHOW FOR SOME TIME...
THE LAST ONE I SAW WAS ABOUT THREE WEEKS AGO...IT WAS PRETTY GOOD, TOO...I REMEMBER ONE SCENE WHERE..
?
SCHULZ

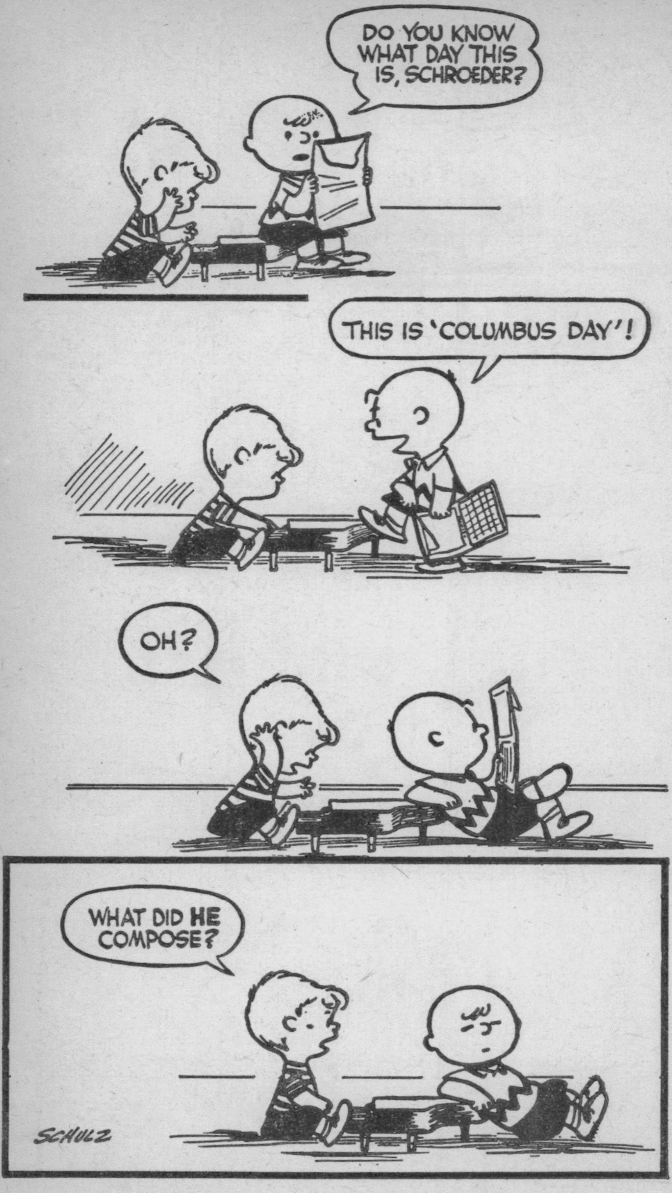

DO YOU KNOW WHAT DAY THIS IS, SCHROEDER?
THIS IS 'COLUMBUS DAY'!
OH?
WHAT DID HE COMPOSE?
SCHULZ

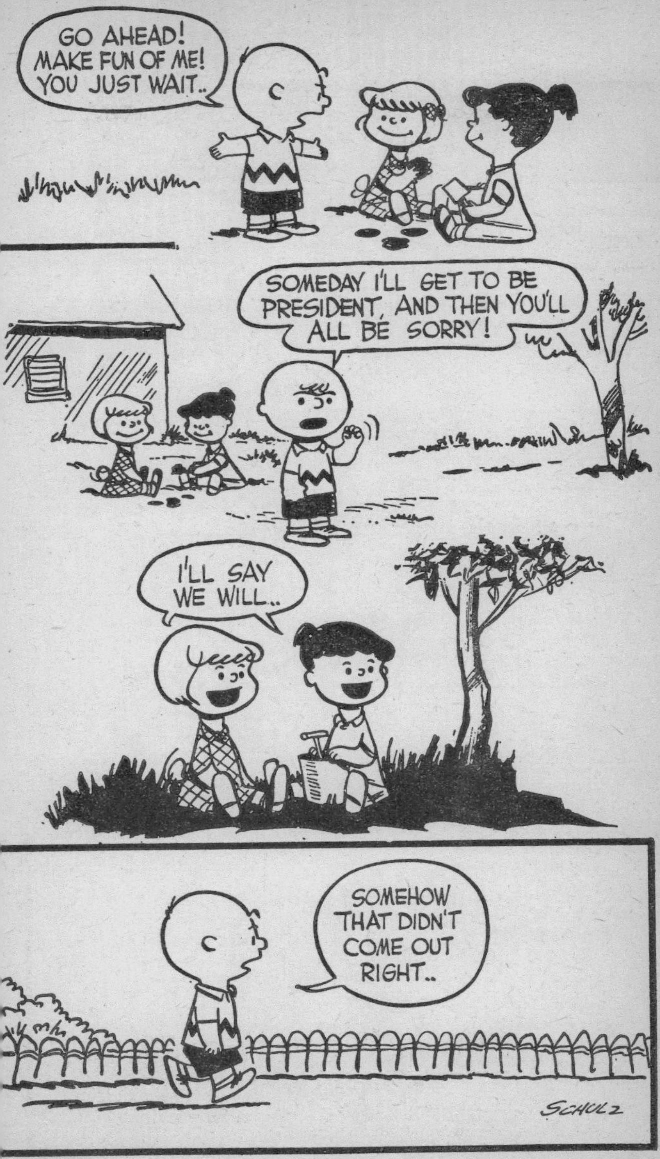
GO AHEAD! MAKE FUN OF ME! YOU JUST WAIT..
SOMEDAY I'LL GET TO BE PRESIDENT, AND THEN YOU'LL ALL BE SORRY!
I'LL SAY WE WILL..
SOMEHOW THAT DIDN'T COME OUT RIGHT..
SCHULZ

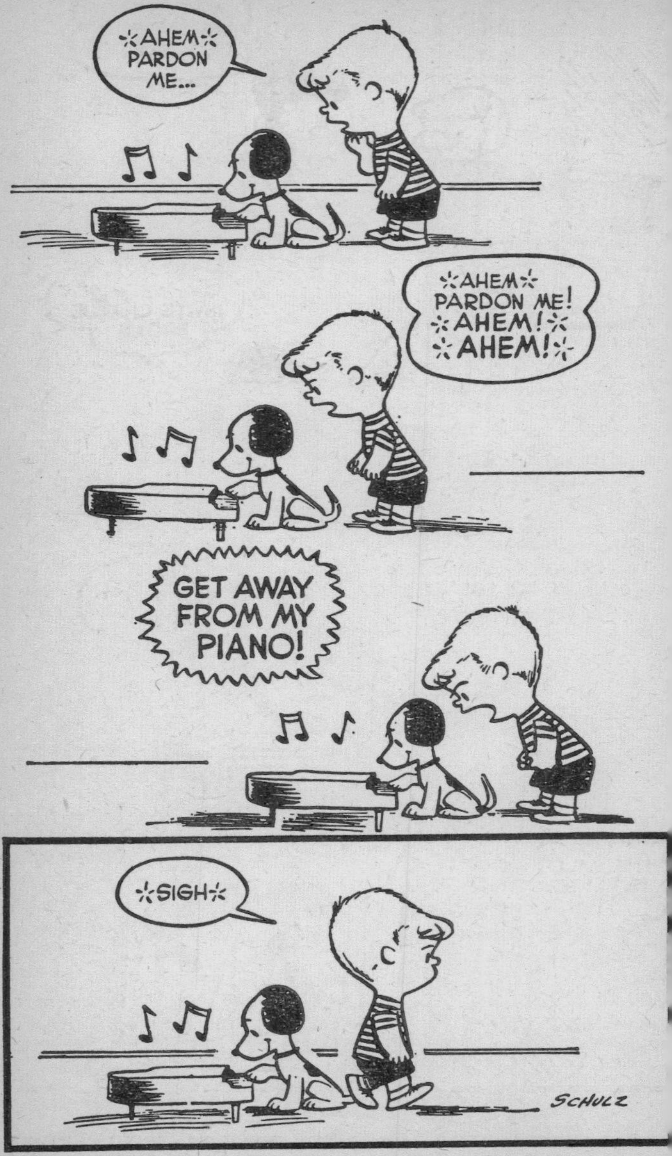
AHEM PARDON ME...
AHEM PARDON ME! *AHEM!* *AHEM!*
GET AWAY FROM MY PIANO!
SIGH
SCHULZ

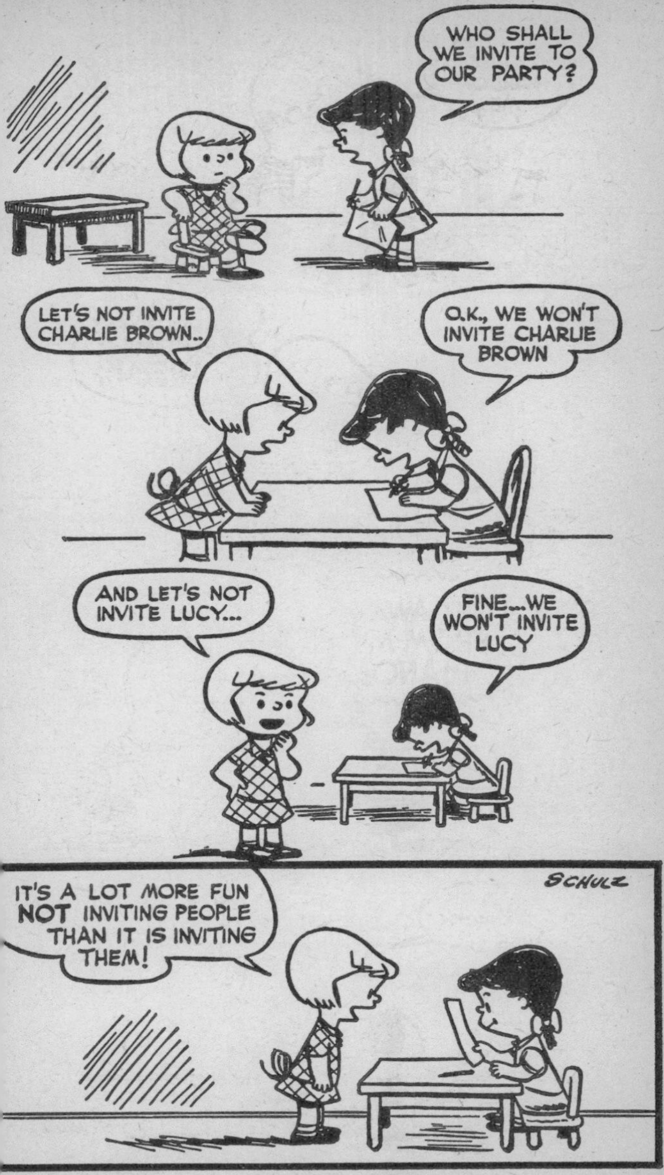
WHO SHALL WE INVITE TO OUR PARTY?
LET'S NOT INVITE CHARLIE BROWN..
O.K., WE WON'T INVITE CHARLIE BROWN
AND LET'S NOT INVITE LUCY...
FINE...WE WON'T INVITE LUCY
SCHULZ
IT'S A LOT MORE FUN NOT INVITING PEOPLE THAN IT IS INVITING THEM!

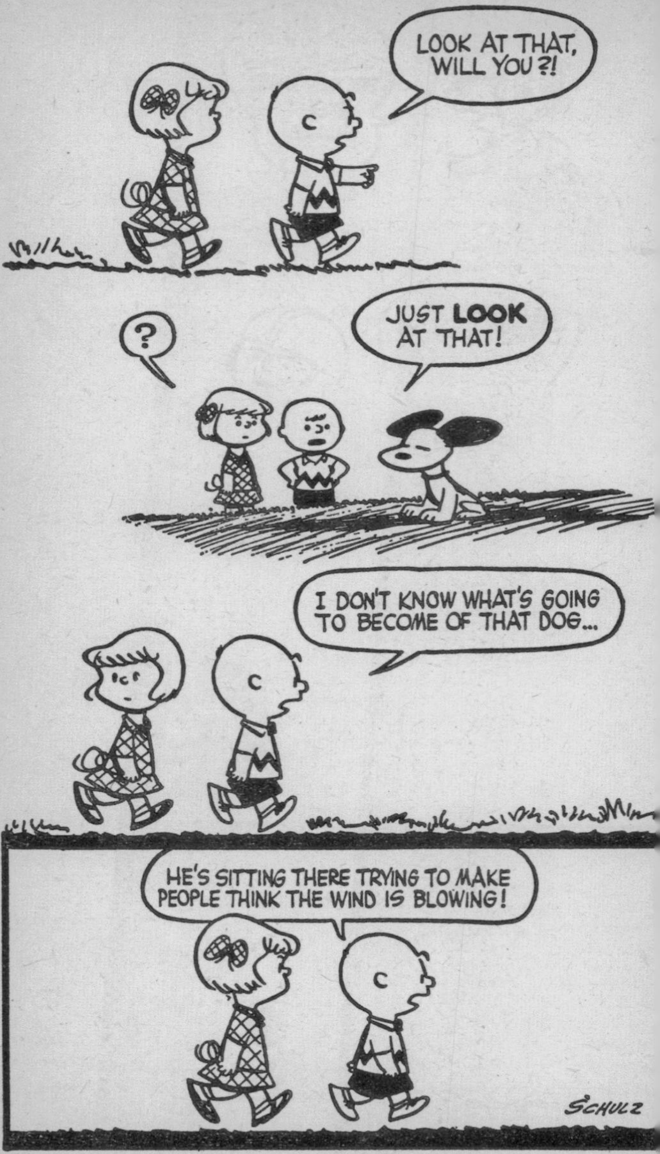

LOOK AT THAT, WILL YOU ?!
?
JUST LOOK AT THAT!
I DON'T KNOW WHAT'S GOING TO BECOME OF THAT DOG...
HE'S SITTING THERE TRYING TO MAKE PEOPLE THINK THE WIND IS BLOWING!
SCHULZ

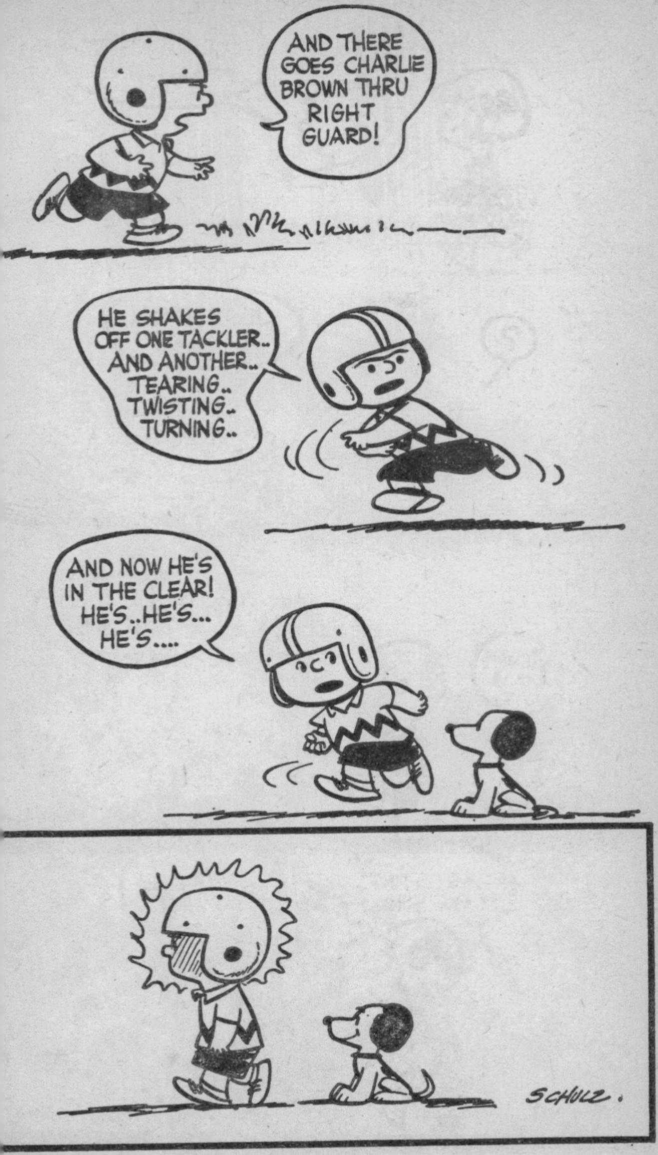
AND THERE GOES CHARLIE BROWN THRU RIGHT GUARD!
HE SHAKES OFF ONE TACKLER.. AND ANOTHER.. TEARING.. TWISTING.. TURNING..
AND NOW HE'S IN THE CLEAR! HE'S..HE'S... HE'S....
SCHULZ

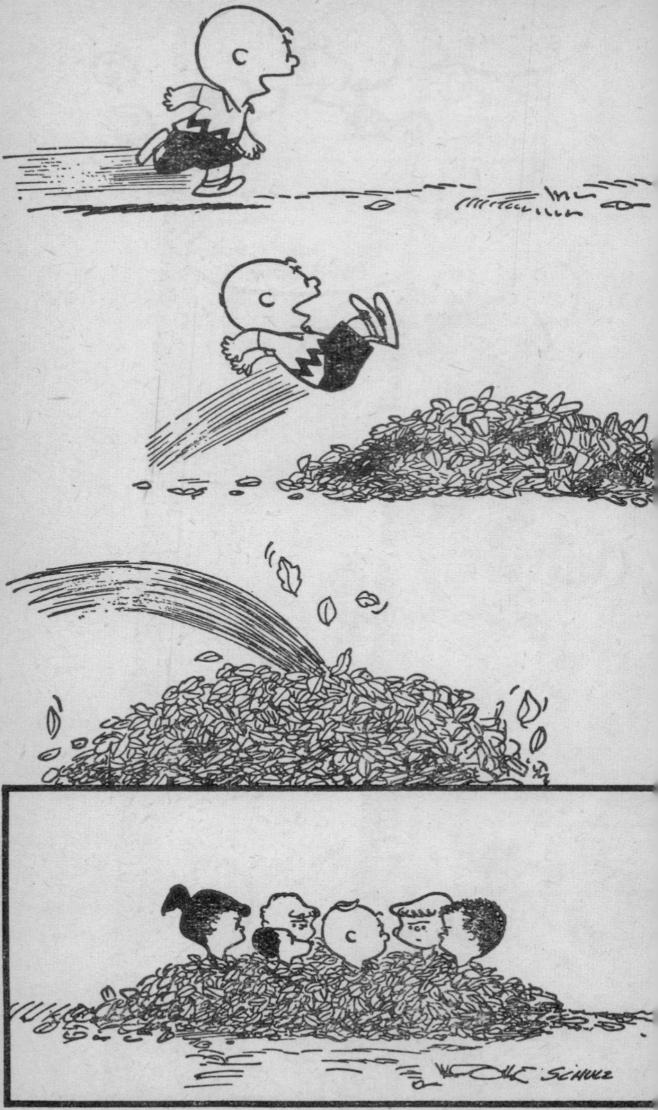
SCHULZ

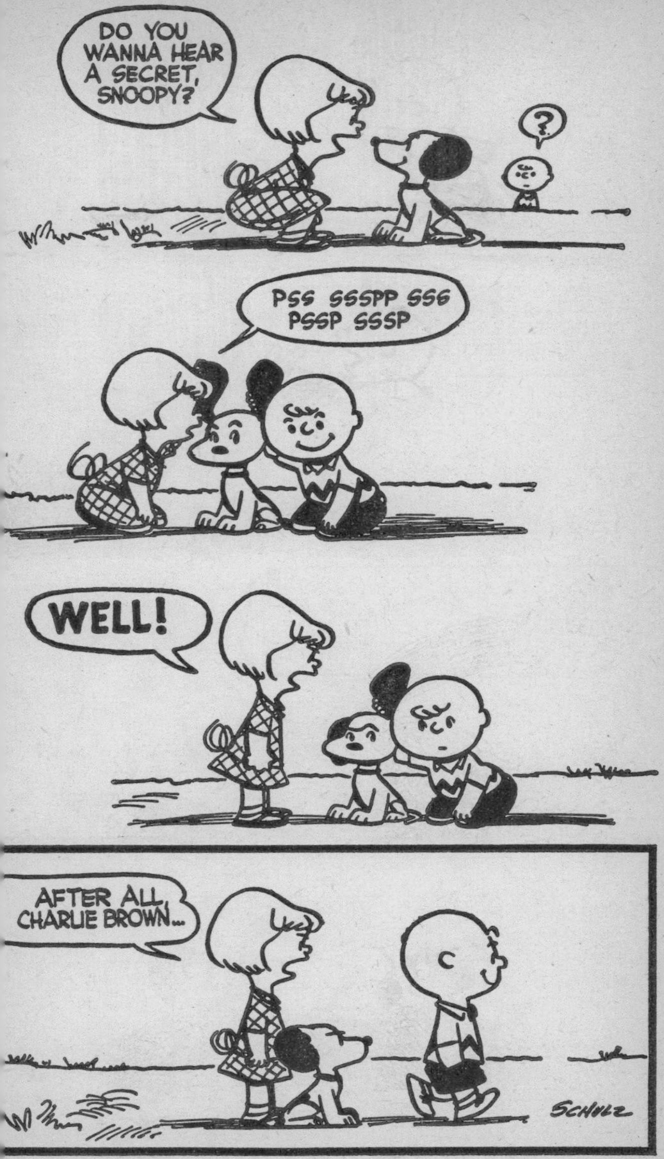
DO YOU WANNA HEAR A SECRET, SNOOPY?
?
PSS SSSPP SSS PSSP SSSP
WELL!
AFTER ALL, CHARLIE BROWN...
SCHULZ

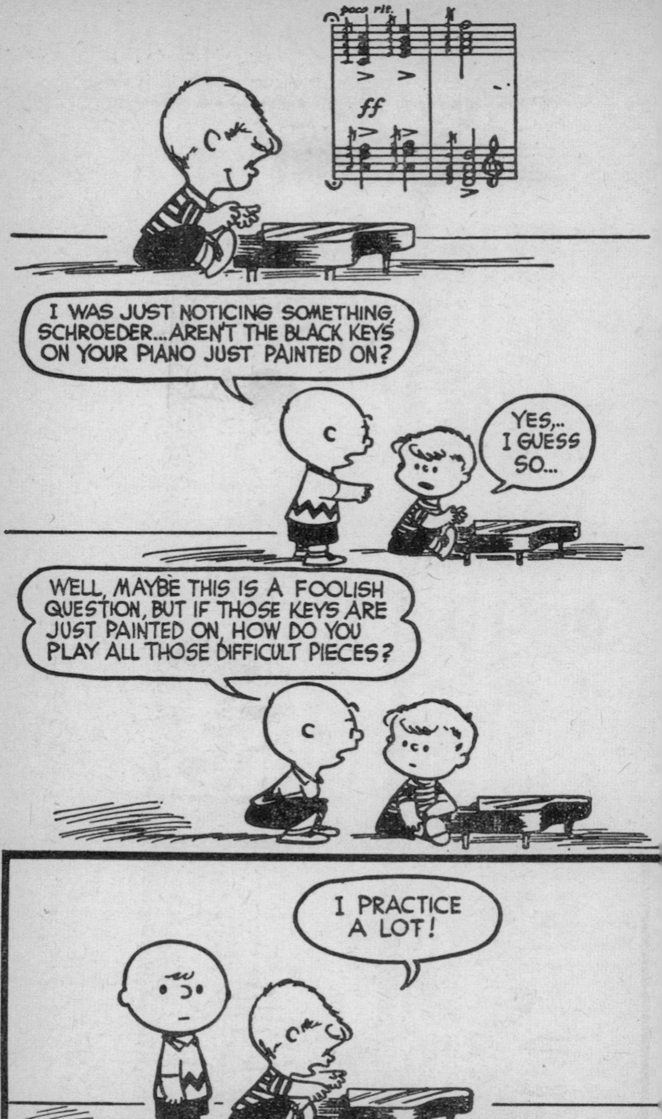
poco rit.
ff
I WAS JUST NOTICING SOMETHING, SCHROEDER...AREN'T THE BLACK KEYS ON YOUR PIANO JUST PAINTED ON?
YES,.. I GUESS SO...
WELL, MAYBE THIS IS A FOOLISH QUESTION, BUT IF THOSE KEYS ARE JUST PAINTED ON, HOW DO YOU PLAY ALL THOSE DIFFICULT PIECES?
I PRACTICE A LOT!
SCHULZ

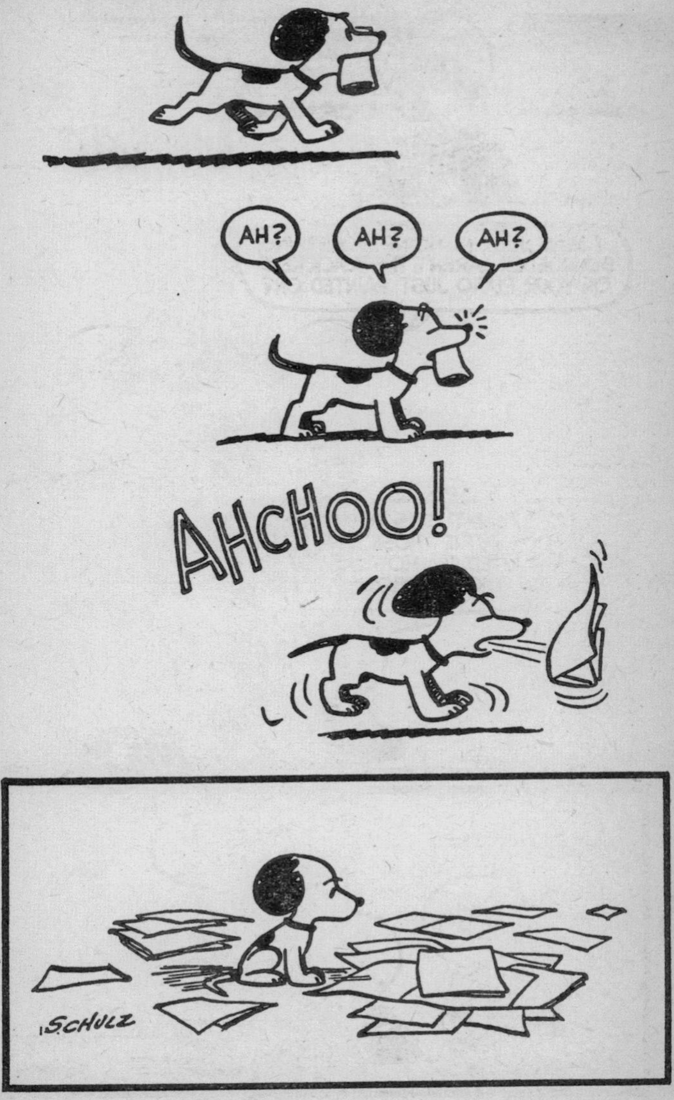

AH?
AH?
AH?
AHCHOO!
S. SCHULZ

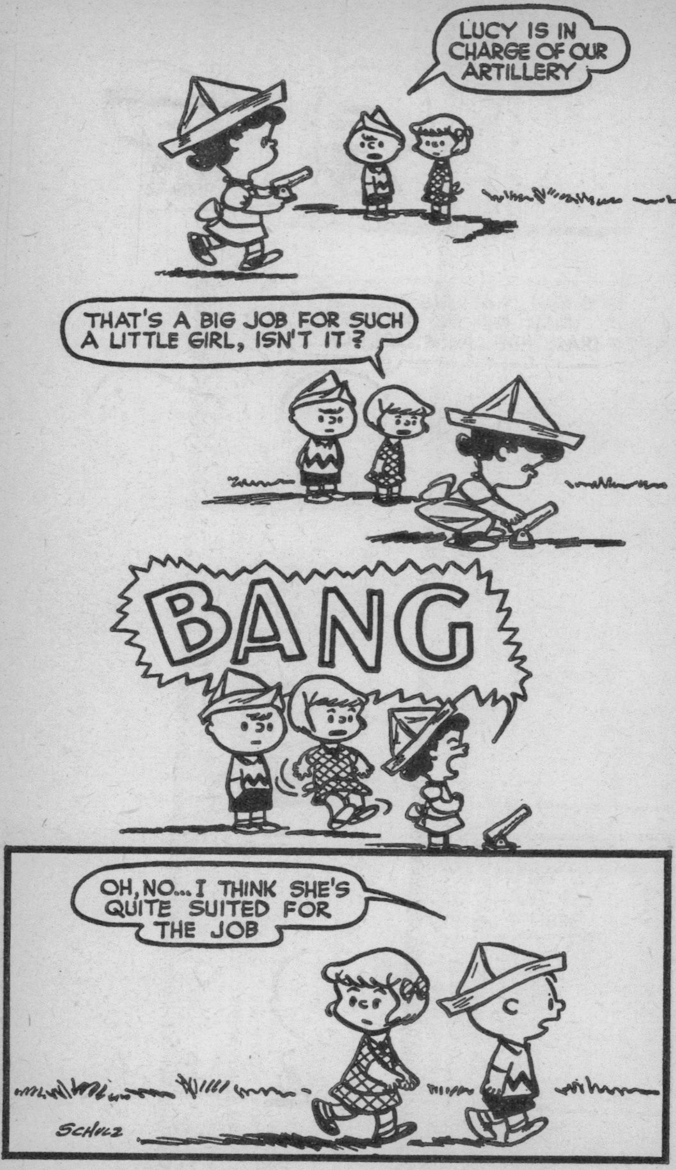
LUCY IS IN CHARGE OF OUR ARTILLERY
THAT'S A BIG JOB FOR SUCH A LITTLE GIRL, ISN'T IT?
BANG
OH, NO...I THINK SHE'S QUITE SUITED FOR THE JOB
SCHULZ

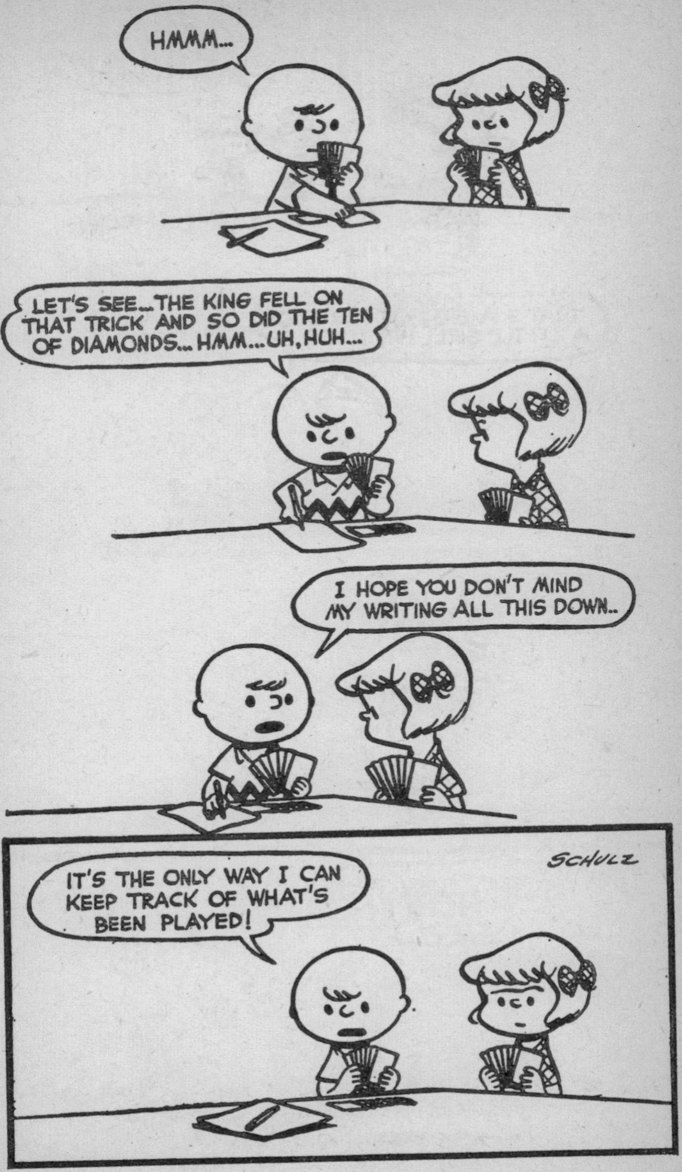
HMMM...
LET'S SEE...THE KING FELL ON THAT TRICK AND SO DID THE TEN OF DIAMONDS... HMM...UH, HUH...
I HOPE YOU DON'T MIND MY WRITING ALL THIS DOWN..
SCHULZ
IT'S THE ONLY WAY I CAN KEEP TRACK OF WHAT'S BEEN PLAYED!

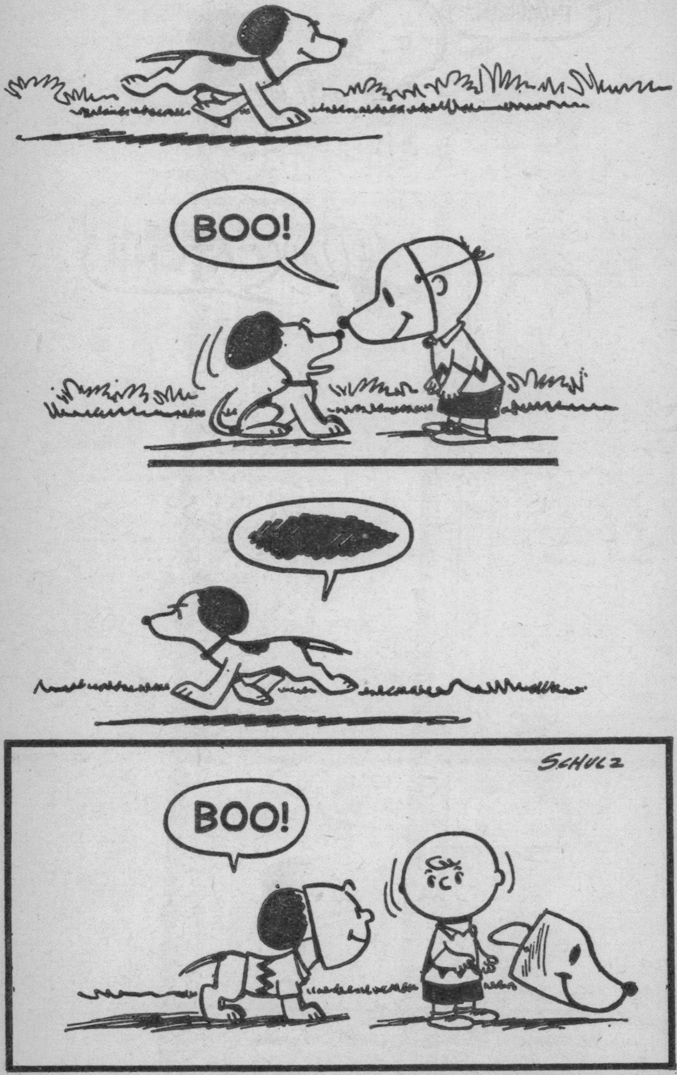
BOO!
SCHULZ
BOO!

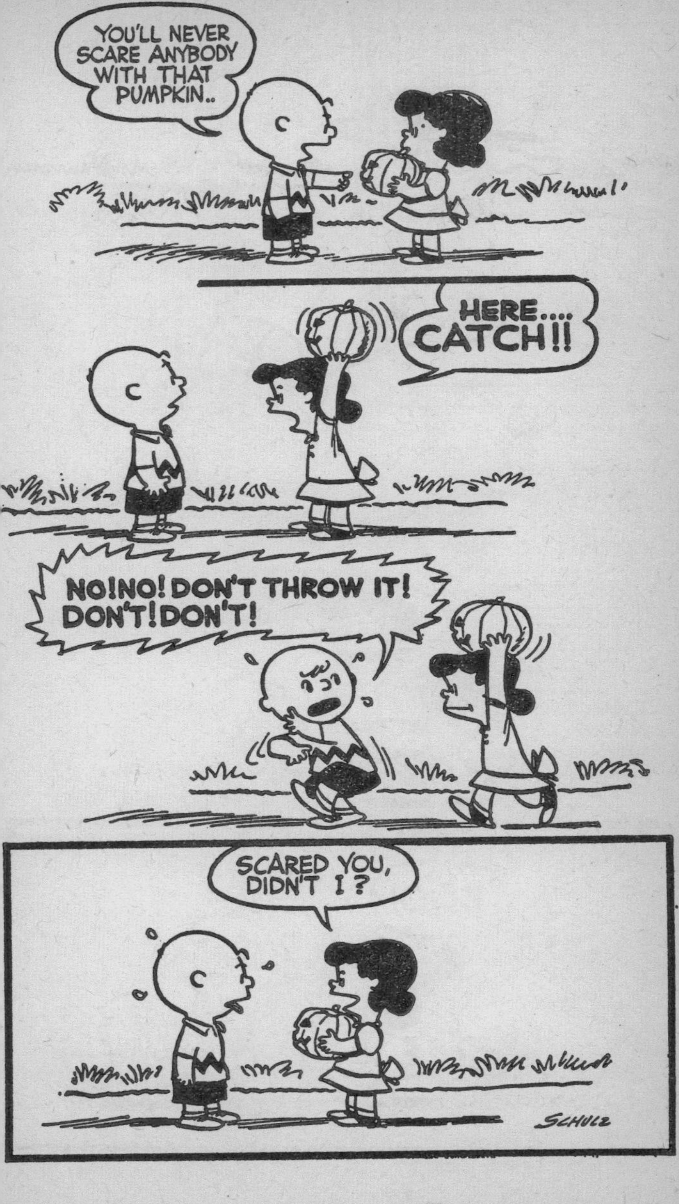
YOU'LL NEVER SCARE ANYBODY WITH THAT PUMPKIN..
HERE.... CATCH!!
NO!NO! DON'T THROW IT! DON'T! DON'T!
SCARED YOU, DIDN'T I?
SCHULZ

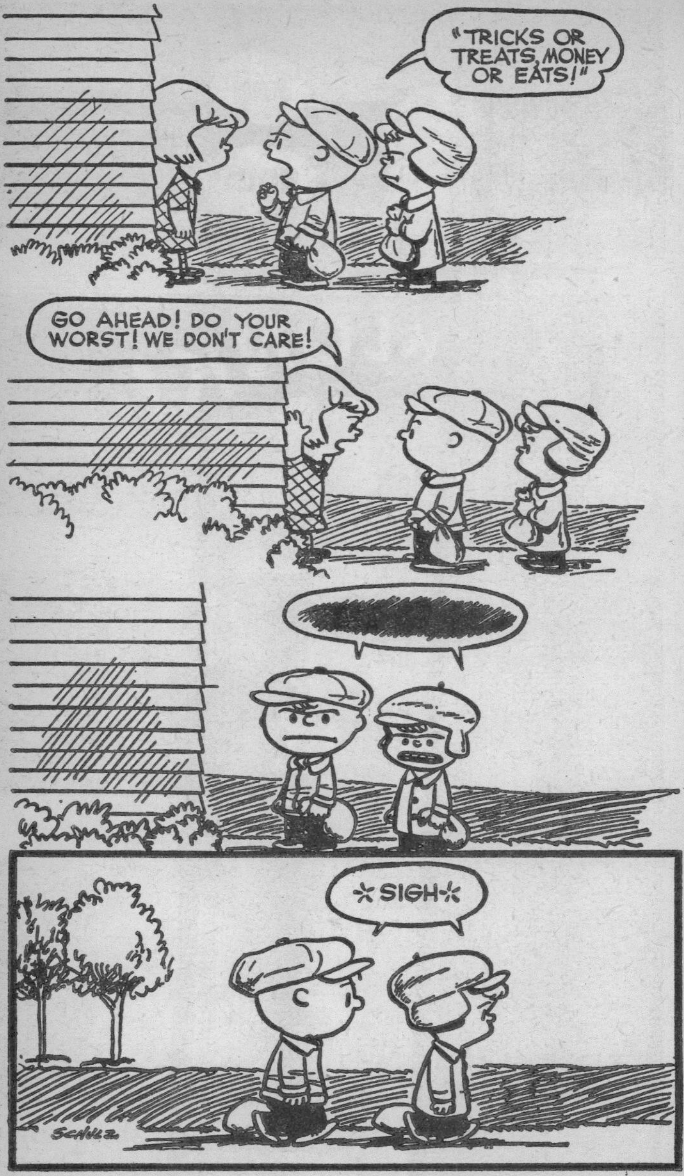
"TRICKS OR TREATS, MONEY OR EATS!"
GO AHEAD! DO YOUR WORST! WE DON'T CARE!
SIGH
SCHULZ

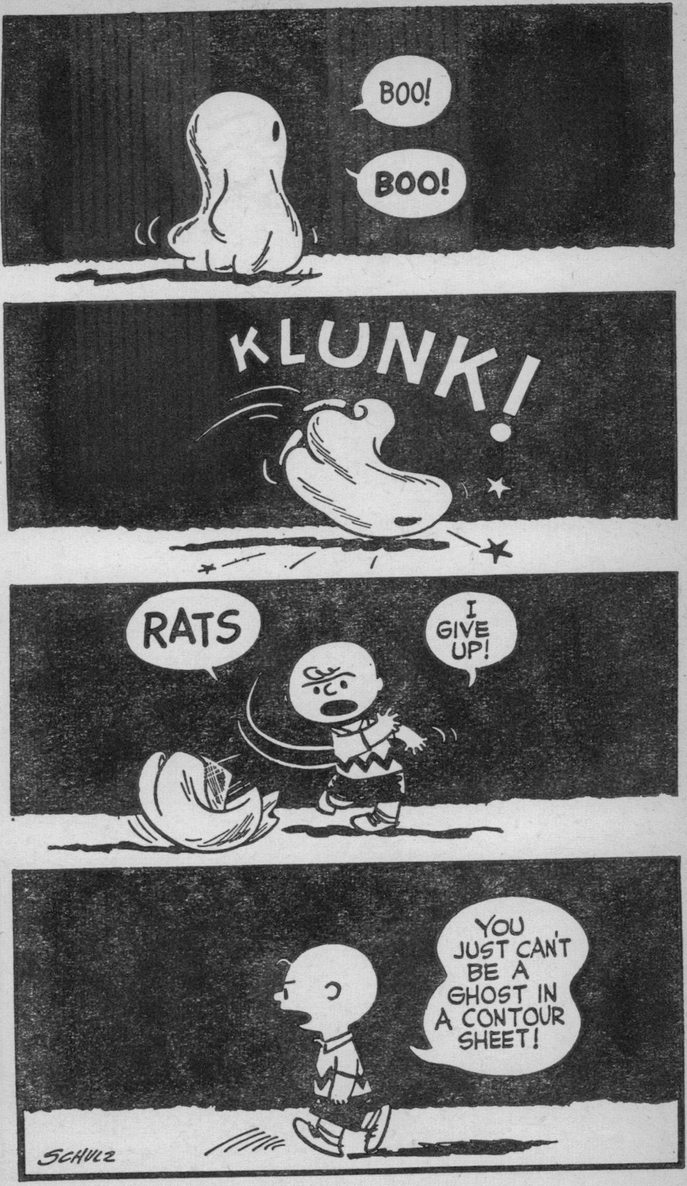
BOO!
BOO!
KLUNK!
RATS
I GIVE UP!
YOU JUST CAN'T BE A GHOST IN A CONTOUR SHEET!
SCHULZ

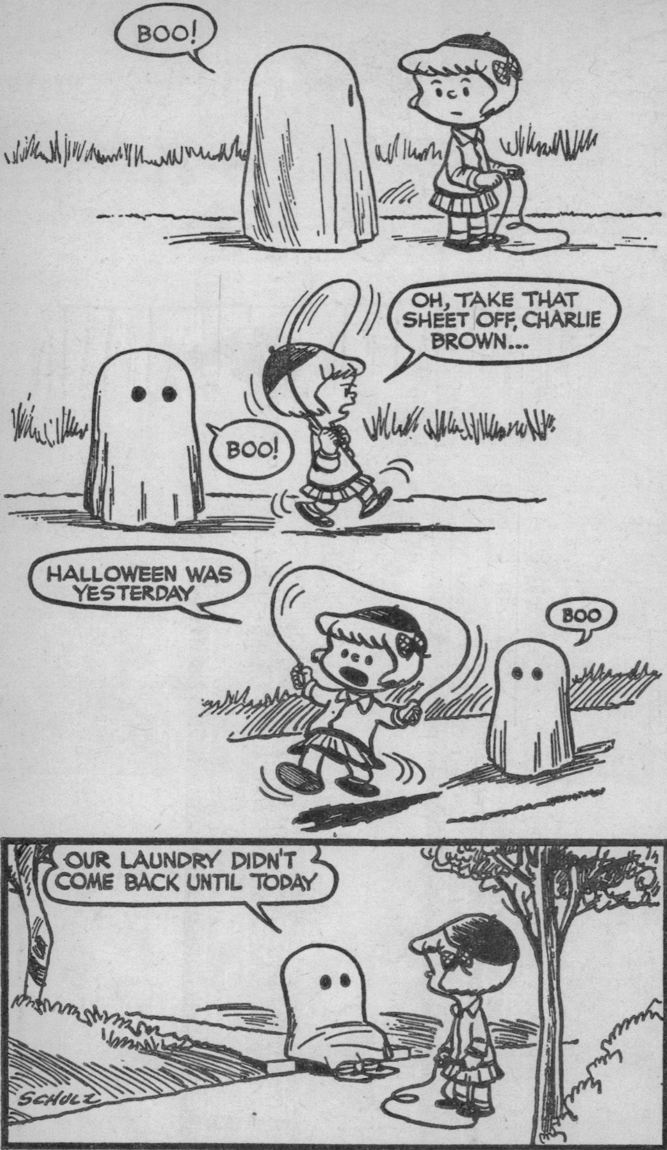
BOO!
OH, TAKE THAT SHEET OFF, CHARLIE BROWN...
BOO!
HALLOWEEN WAS YESTERDAY
BOO
OUR LAUNDRY DIDN'T COME BACK UNTIL TODAY
SCHULZ

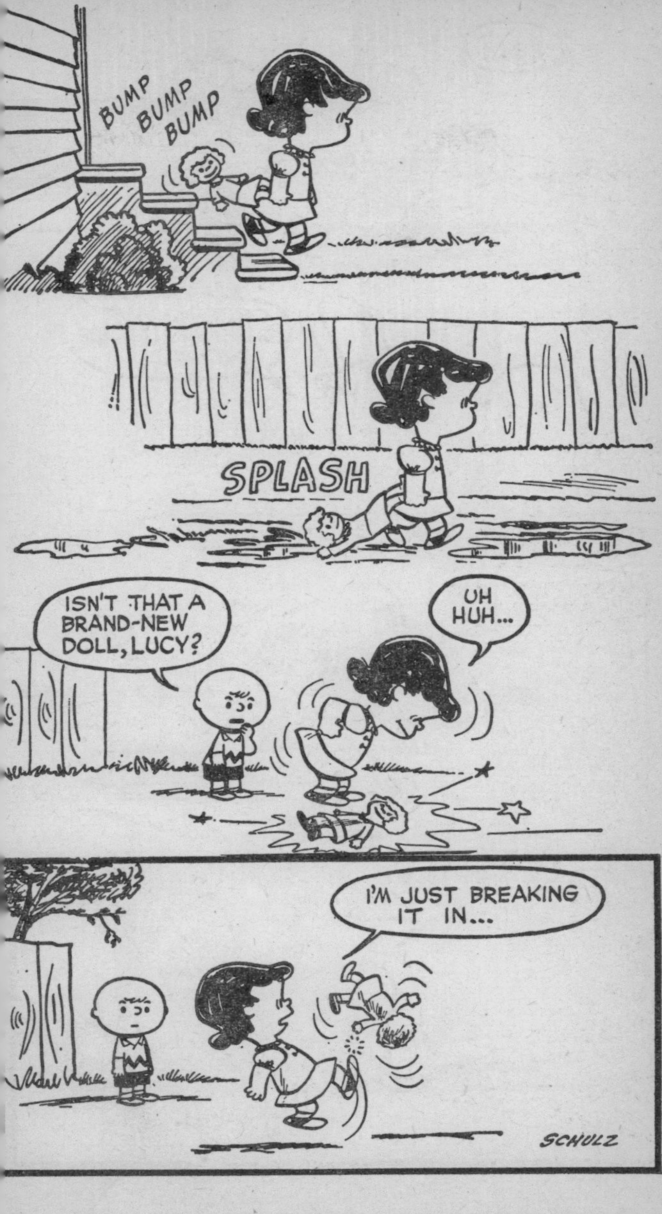
BUMP
BUMP
BUMP
SPLASH
ISN'T THAT A BRAND-NEW DOLL, LUCY?
UH HUH...
I'M JUST BREAKING IT IN...
SCHULZ

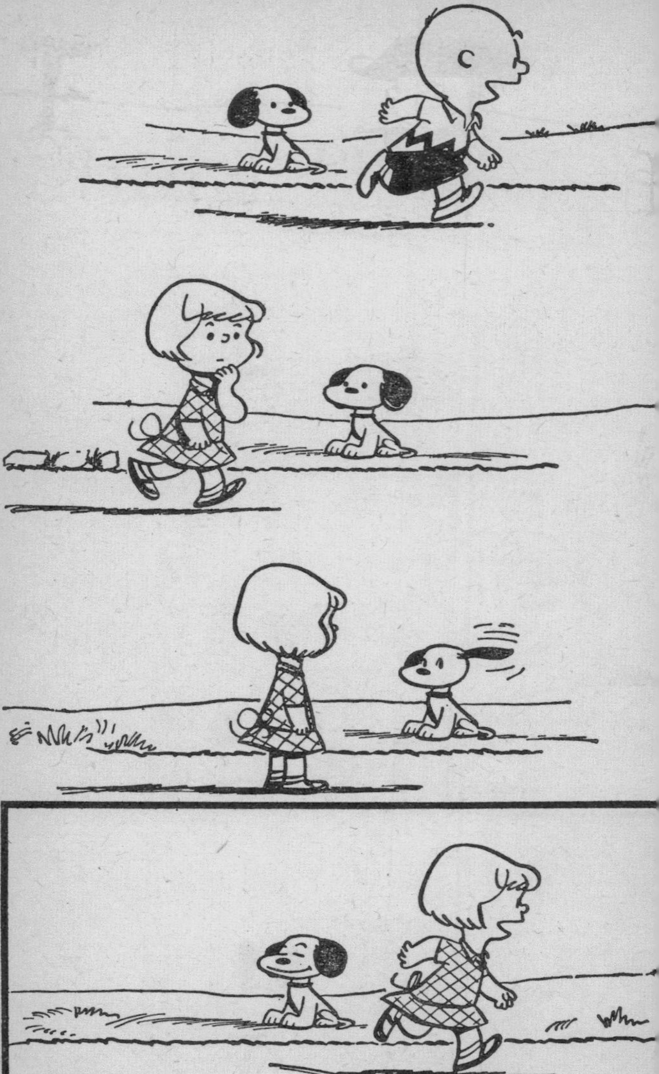
SCHULZ

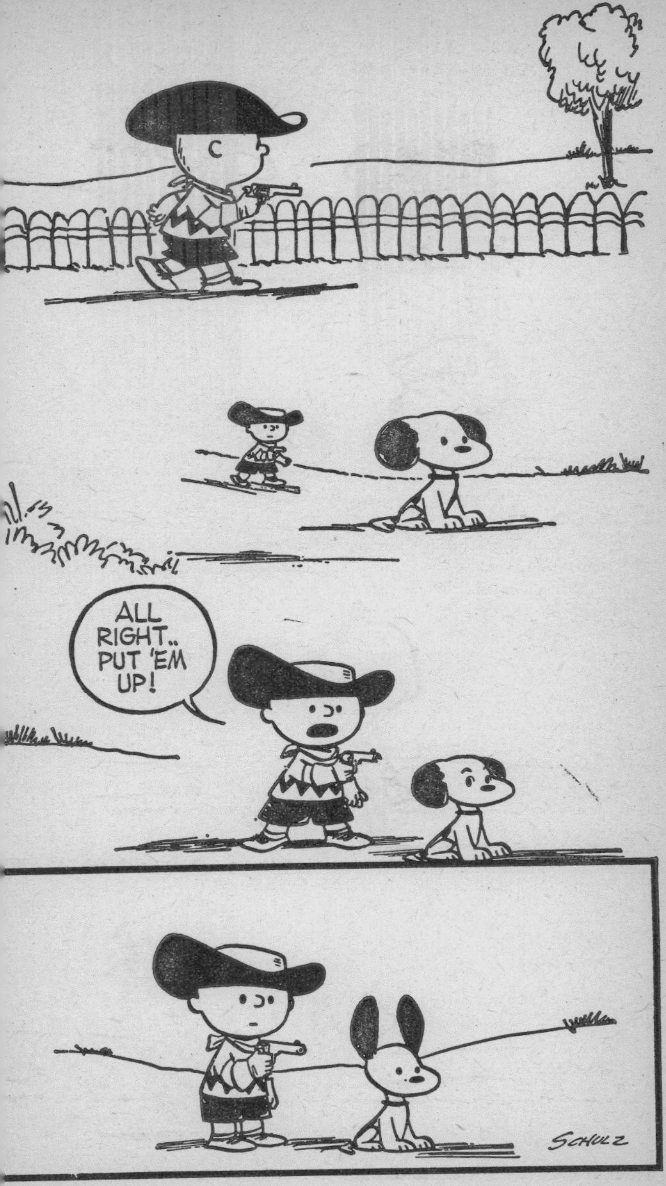
ALL RIGHT.. PUT 'EM UP!
SCHULZ

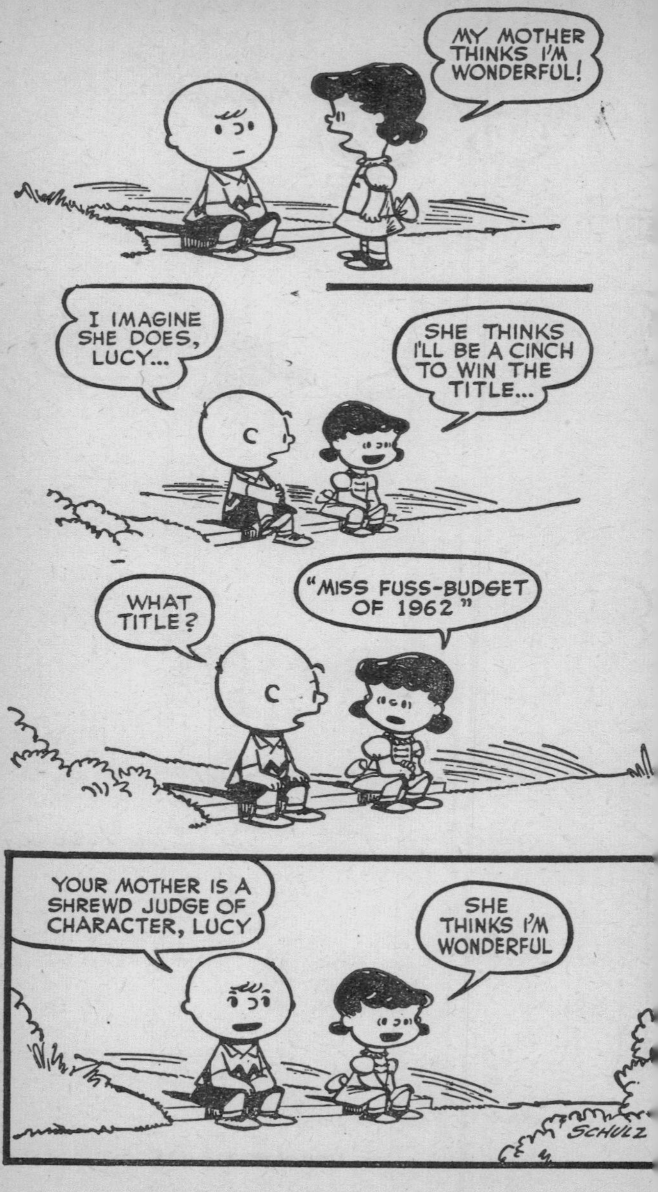
MY MOTHER THINKS I'M WONDERFUL!
I IMAGINE SHE DOES, LUCY...
SHE THINKS I'LL BE A CINCH TO WIN THE TITLE...
WHAT TITLE?
"MISS FUSS-BUDGET OF 1962"
YOUR MOTHER IS A SHREWD JUDGE OF CHARACTER, LUCY
SHE THINKS I'M WONDERFUL
SCHULZ

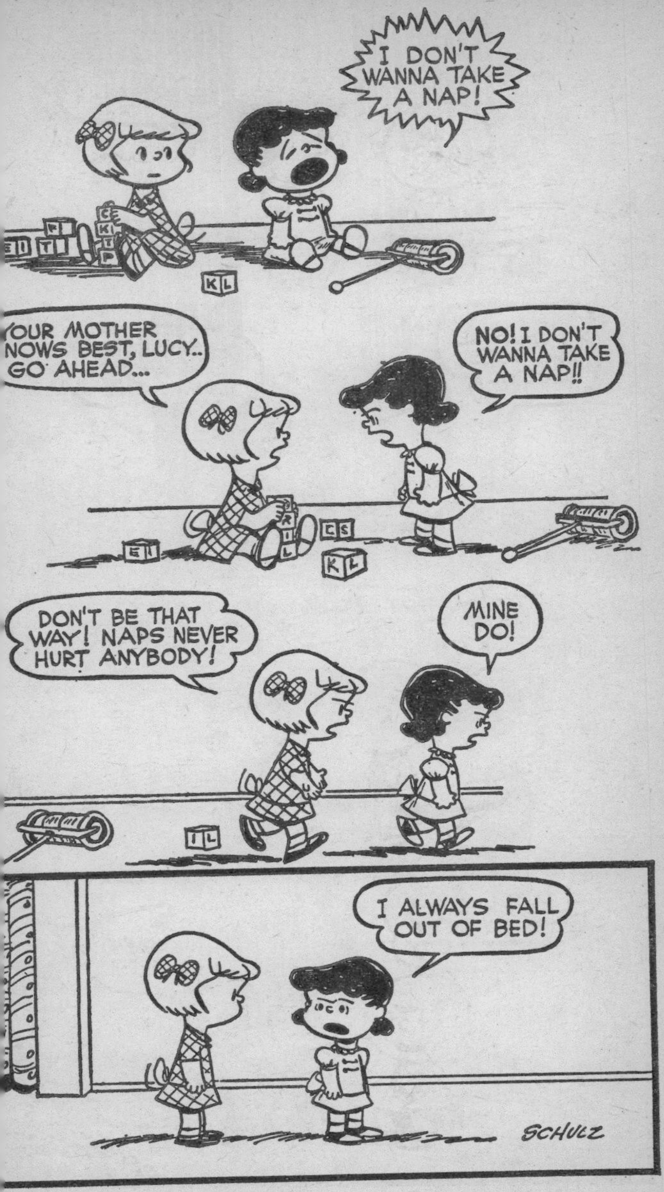
I DON'T WANNA TAKE A NAP!
YOUR MOTHER NOWS BEST, LUCY.. GO AHEAD...
NO! I DON'T WANNA TAKE A NAP!!
DON'T BE THAT WAY! NAPS NEVER HURT ANYBODY!
MINE DO!
I ALWAYS FALL OUT OF BED!
SCHULZ

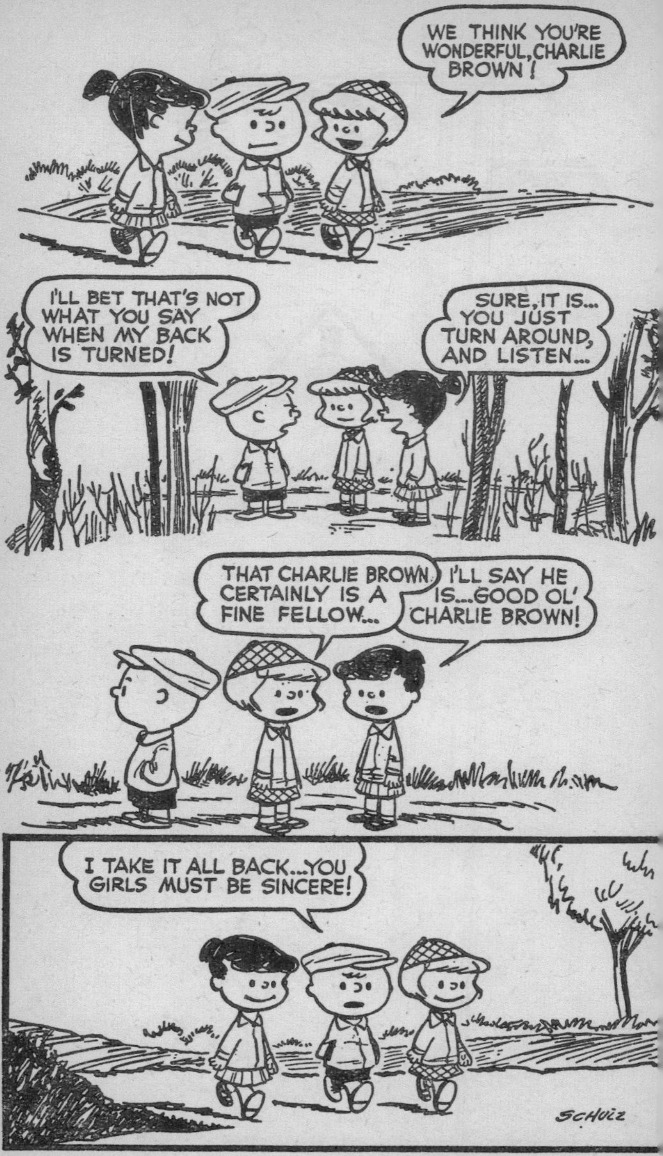
WE THINK YOU'RE WONDERFUL, CHARLIE BROWN!
I'LL BET THAT'S NOT WHAT YOU SAY WHEN MY BACK IS TURNED!
SURE, IT IS... YOU JUST TURN AROUND, AND LISTEN...
THAT CHARLIE BROWN CERTAINLY IS A FINE FELLOW...
I'LL SAY HE IS...GOOD OL' CHARLIE BROWN!
I TAKE IT ALL BACK...YOU GIRLS MUST BE SINCERE!
SCHULZ

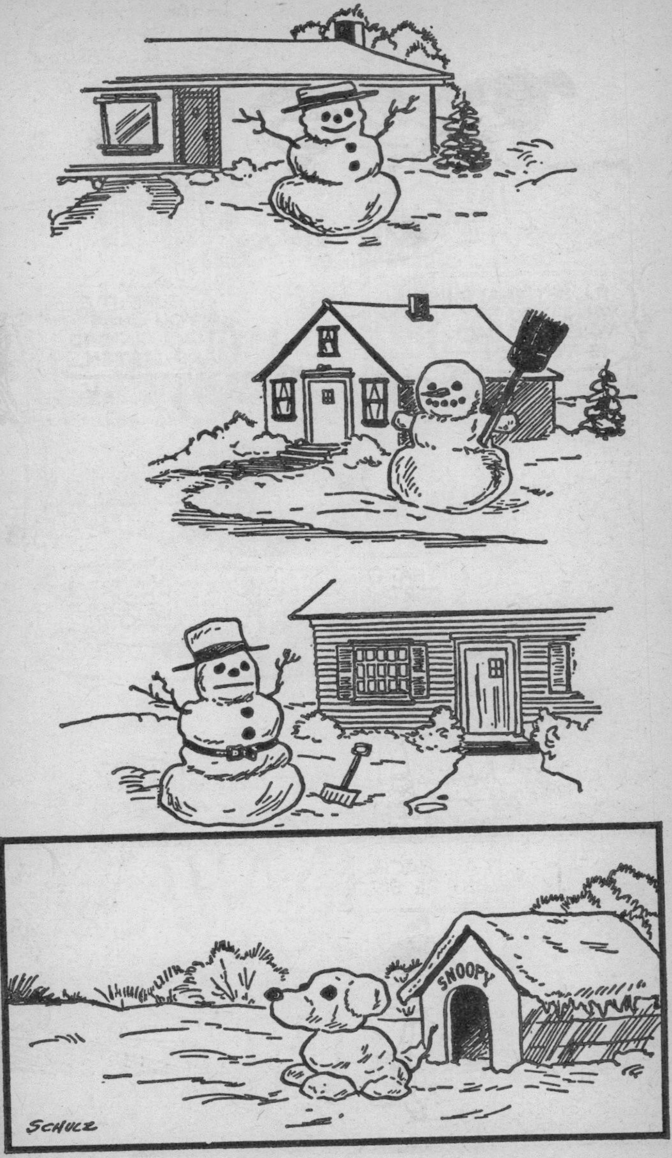
SNOOPY
SCHULZ

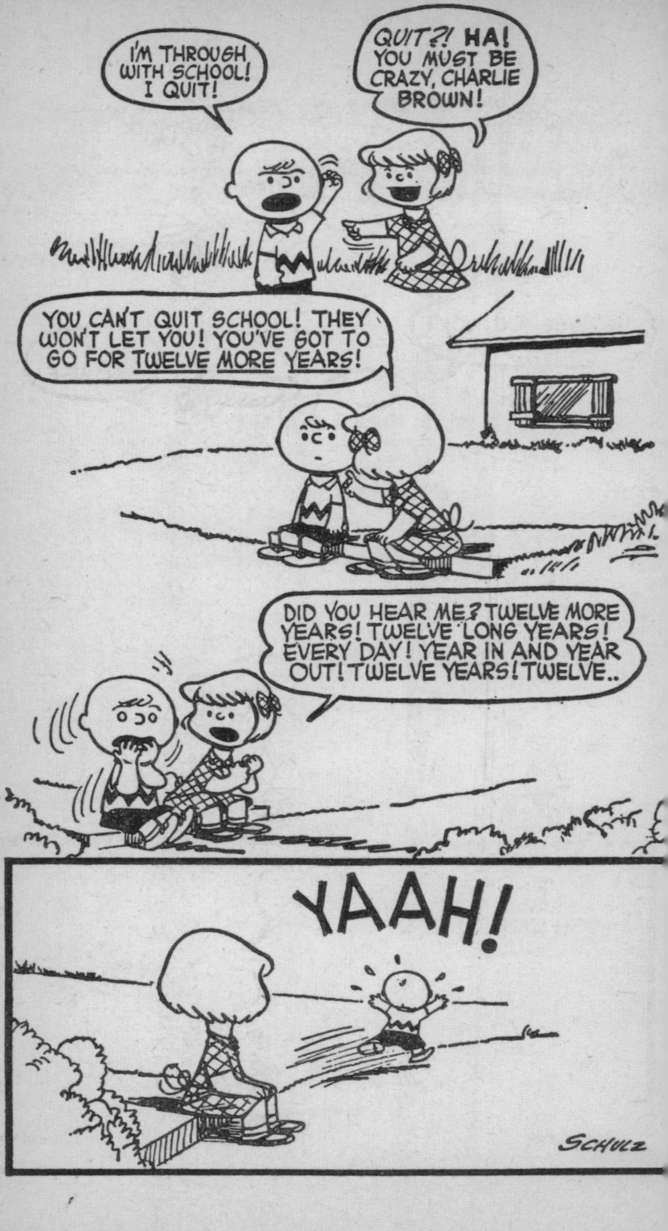
I'M THROUGH WITH SCHOOL! I QUIT!
QUIT?! HA! YOU MUST BE CRAZY, CHARLIE BROWN!
YOU CAN'T QUIT SCHOOL! THEY WON'T LET YOU! YOU'VE GOT TO GO FOR TWELVE MORE YEARS!
DID YOU HEAR ME? TWELVE MORE YEARS! TWELVE LONG YEARS! EVERY DAY! YEAR IN AND YEAR OUT! TWELVE YEARS! TWELVE..
YAAH!
SCHULZ

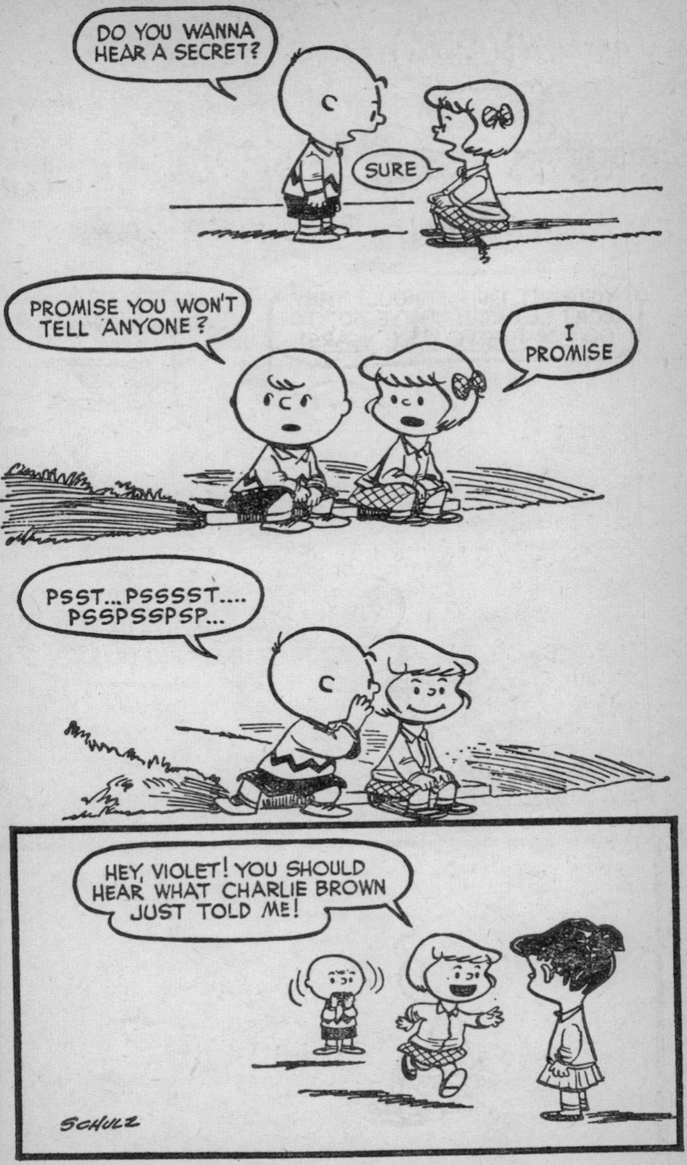
DO YOU WANNA HEAR A SECRET?
SURE
PROMISE YOU WON'T TELL ANYONE?
I PROMISE
PSST...PSSSST.... PSSPSSPSP...
HEY, VIOLET! YOU SHOULD HEAR WHAT CHARLIE BROWN JUST TOLD ME!
SCHULZ

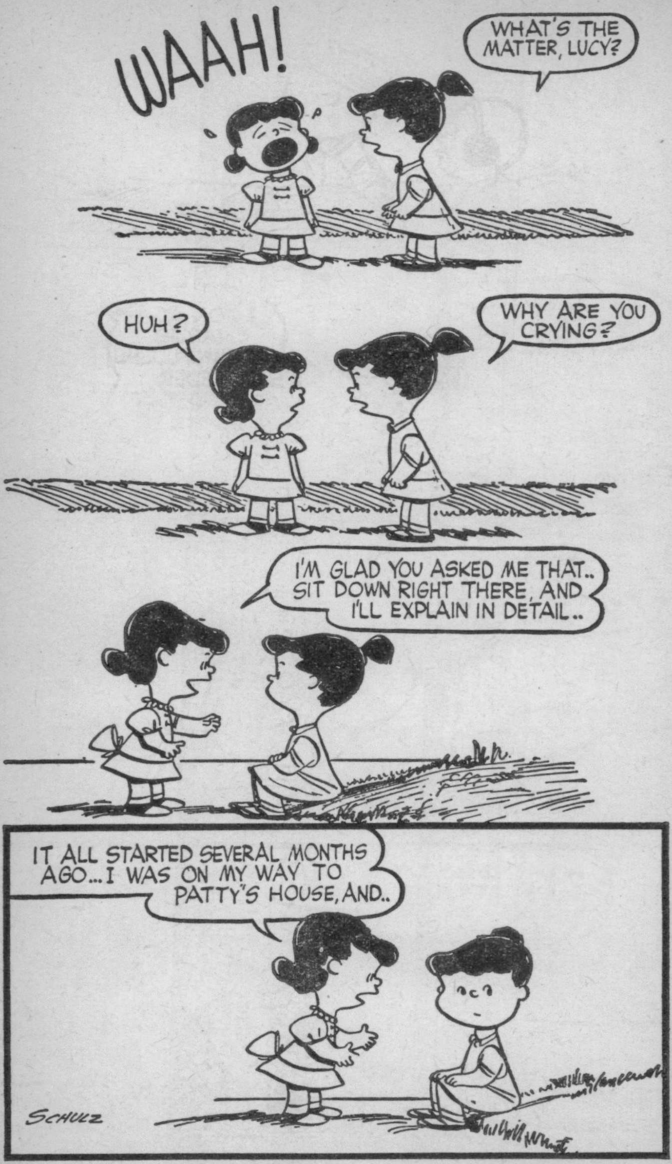
WAAH!
WHAT'S THE MATTER, LUCY?
HUH?
WHY ARE YOU CRYING?
I'M GLAD YOU ASKED ME THAT.. SIT DOWN RIGHT THERE, AND I'LL EXPLAIN IN DETAIL..
IT ALL STARTED SEVERAL MONTHS AGO...I WAS ON MY WAY TO PATTY'S HOUSE, AND..
SCHULZ

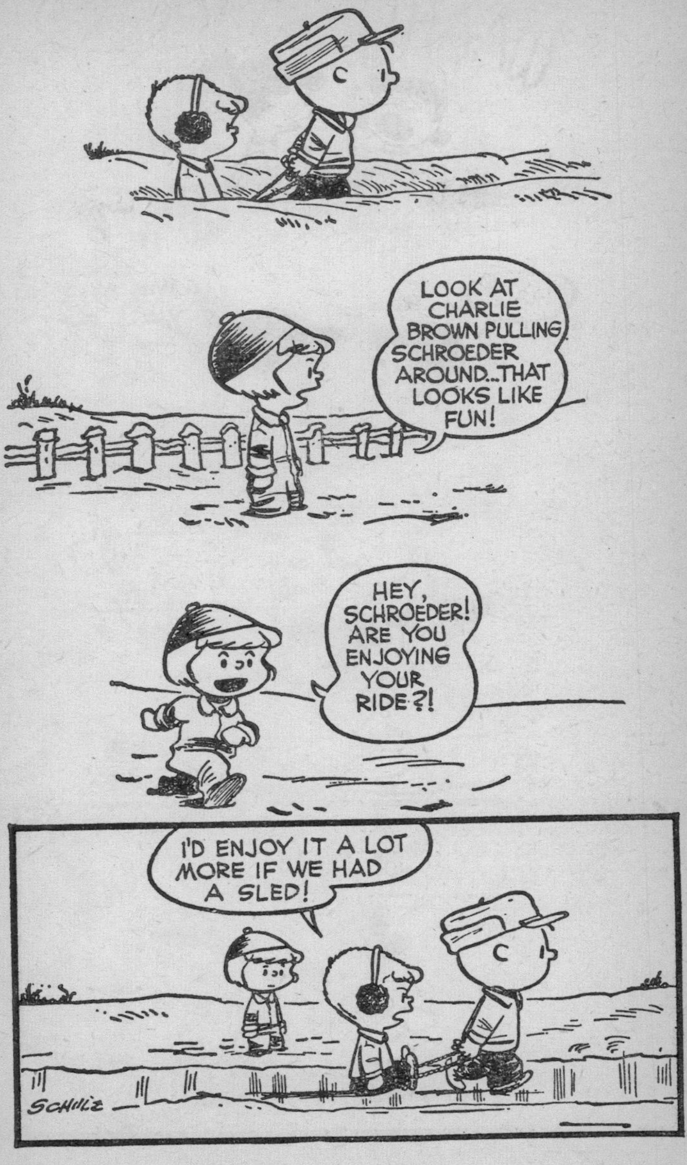
LOOK AT CHARLIE BROWN PULLING SCHROEDER AROUND...THAT LOOKS LIKE FUN!
HEY, SCHROEDER! ARE YOU ENJOYING YOUR RIDE?!
I'D ENJOY IT A LOT MORE IF WE HAD A SLED!
SCHULZ

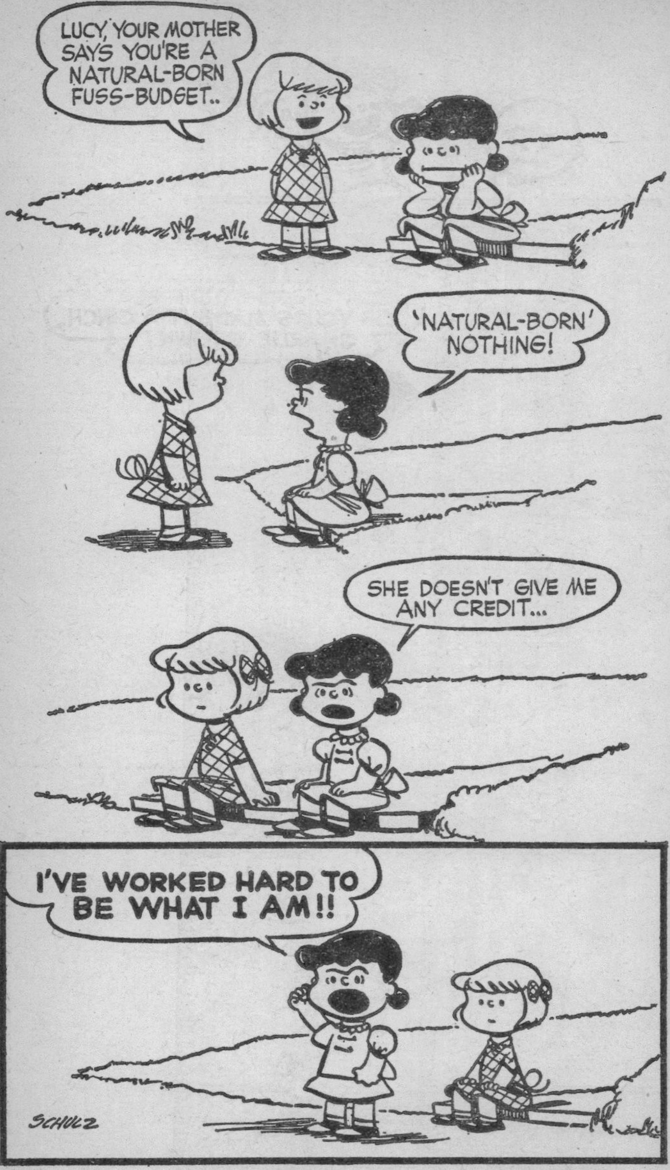
LUCY, YOUR MOTHER SAYS YOU'RE A NATURAL-BORN FUSS-BUDGET..
'NATURAL-BORN' NOTHING!
SHE DOESN'T GIVE ME ANY CREDIT...
I'VE WORKED HARD TO BE WHAT I AM!!
SCHULZ

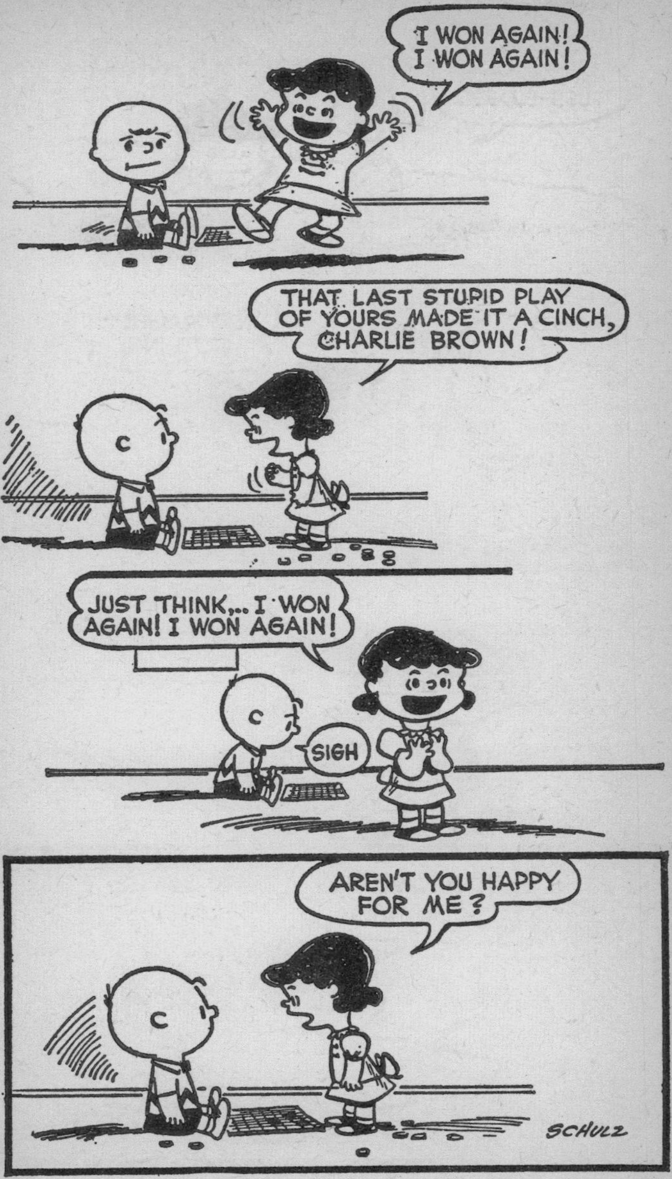
I WON AGAIN! I WON AGAIN!
THAT LAST STUPID PLAY OF YOURS MADE IT A CINCH, CHARLIE BROWN!
JUST THINK,... I WON AGAIN! I WON AGAIN!
SIGH
AREN'T YOU HAPPY FOR ME?
SCHULZ

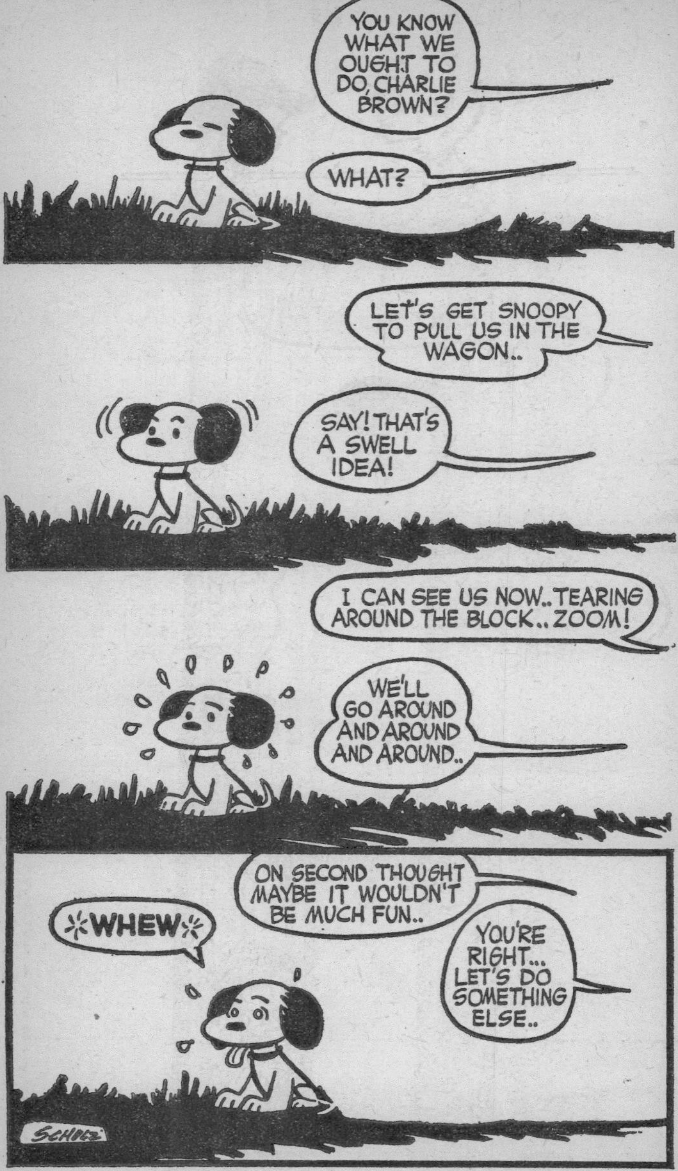
YOU KNOW WHAT WE OUGHT TO DO, CHARLIE BROWN?
WHAT?
LET'S GET SNOOPY TO PULL US IN THE WAGON..
SAY! THAT'S A SWELL IDEA!
I CAN SEE US NOW..TEARING AROUND THE BLOCK..ZOOM!
WE'LL GO AROUND AND AROUND AND AROUND..
ON SECOND THOUGHT MAYBE IT WOULDN'T BE MUCH FUN..
WHEW
YOU'RE RIGHT... LET'S DO SOMETHING ELSE..
SCHULZ

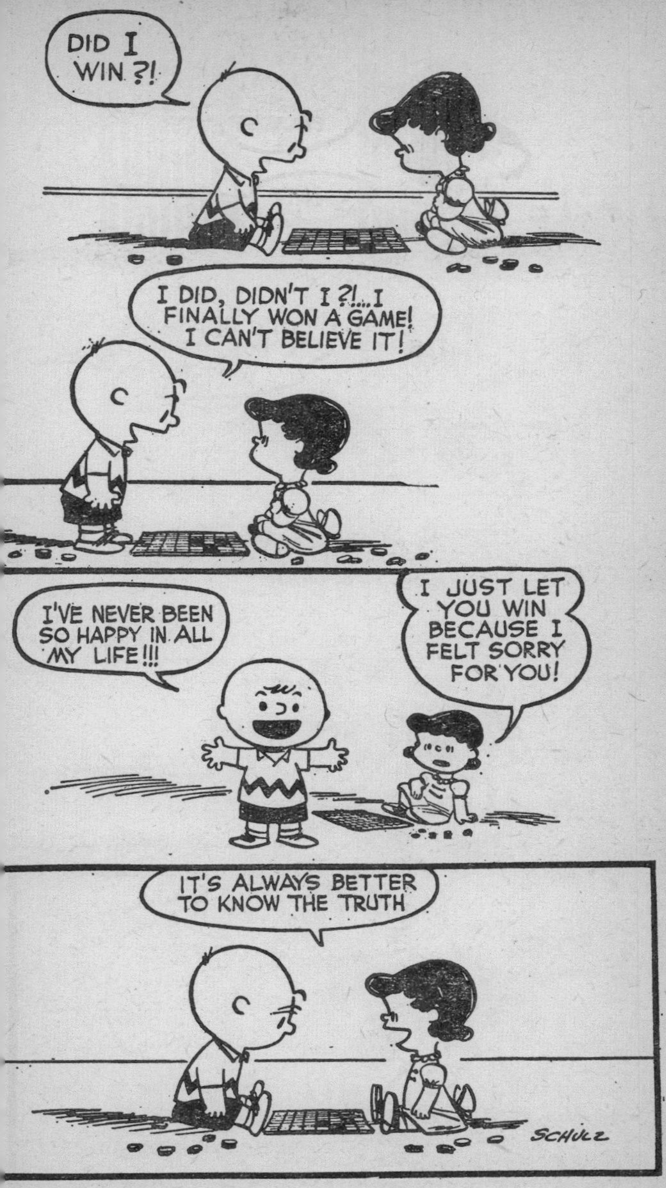

DID I WIN ?!
I DID, DIDN'T I ?!...I FINALLY WON A GAME! I CAN'T BELIEVE IT!
I'VE NEVER BEEN SO HAPPY IN ALL MY LIFE!!!
I JUST LET YOU WIN BECAUSE I FELT SORRY FOR YOU!
IT'S ALWAYS BETTER TO KNOW THE TRUTH
SCHULZ

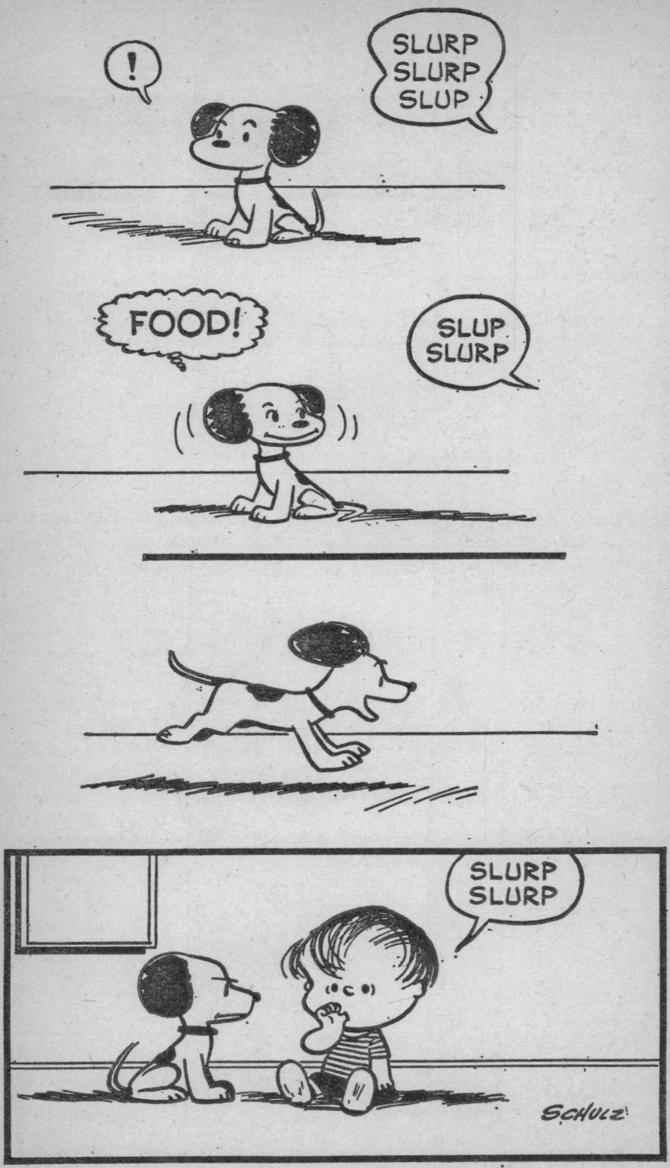
!
SLURP SLURP SLUP
FOOD!
SLUP SLURP
SLURP SLURP
SCHULZ

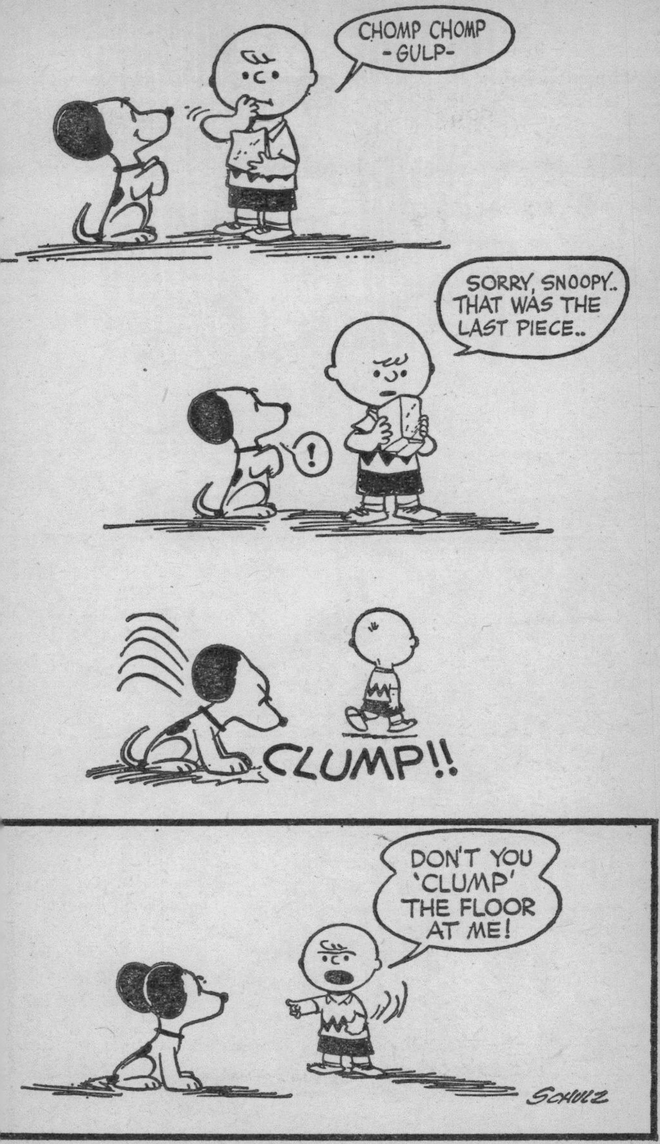
CHOMP CHOMP -GULP-
SORRY, SNOOPY.. THAT WAS THE LAST PIECE..
!
CLUMP!!
DON'T YOU 'CLUMP' THE FLOOR AT ME!
SCHULZ

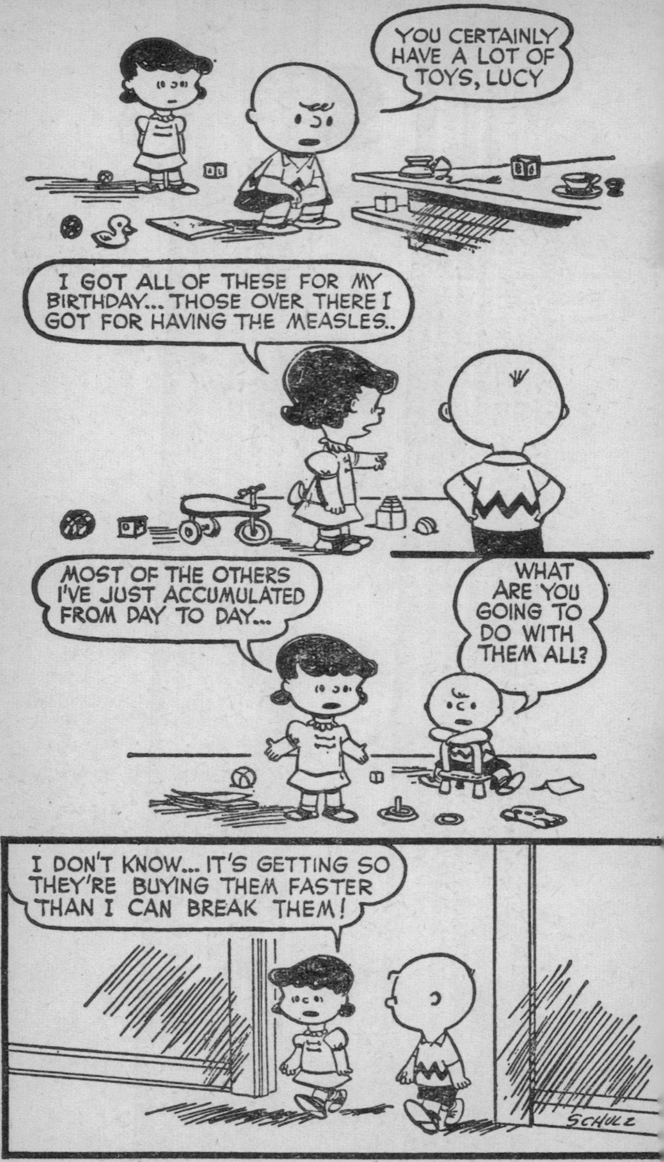
YOU CERTAINLY HAVE A LOT OF TOYS, LUCY
I GOT ALL OF THESE FOR MY BIRTHDAY... THOSE OVER THERE I GOT FOR HAVING THE MEASLES..
MOST OF THE OTHERS I'VE JUST ACCUMULATED FROM DAY TO DAY...
WHAT ARE YOU GOING TO DO WITH THEM ALL?
I DON'T KNOW... IT'S GETTING SO THEY'RE BUYING THEM FASTER THAN I CAN BREAK THEM!
SCHULZ

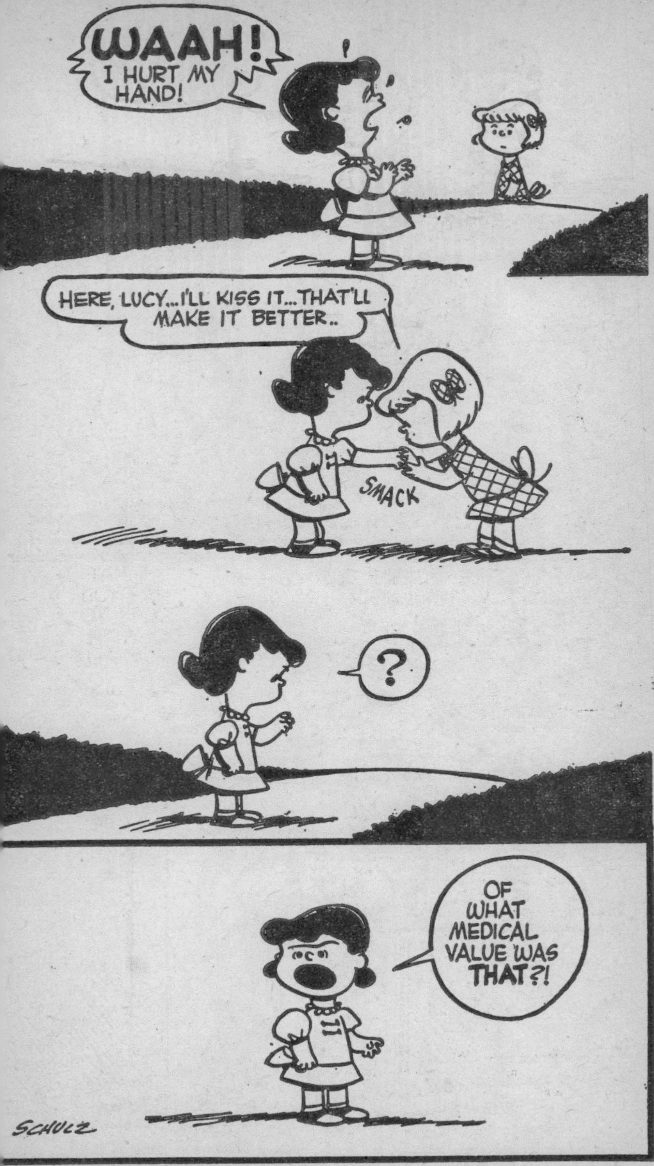
WAAH! I HURT MY HAND!
HERE, LUCY...I'LL KISS IT...THAT'LL MAKE IT BETTER..
SMACK
?
OF WHAT MEDICAL VALUE WAS THAT?!
SCHULZ

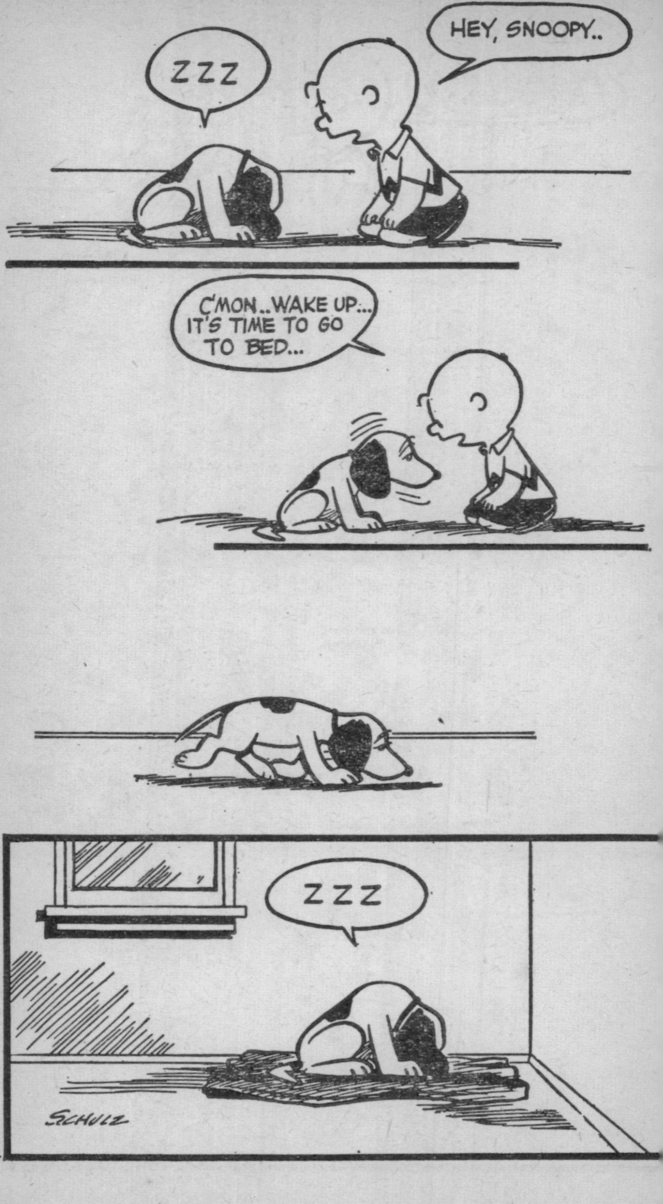
HEY, SNOOPY..
ZZZ
C'MON..WAKE UP... IT'S TIME TO GO TO BED...
ZZZ
SCHULZ

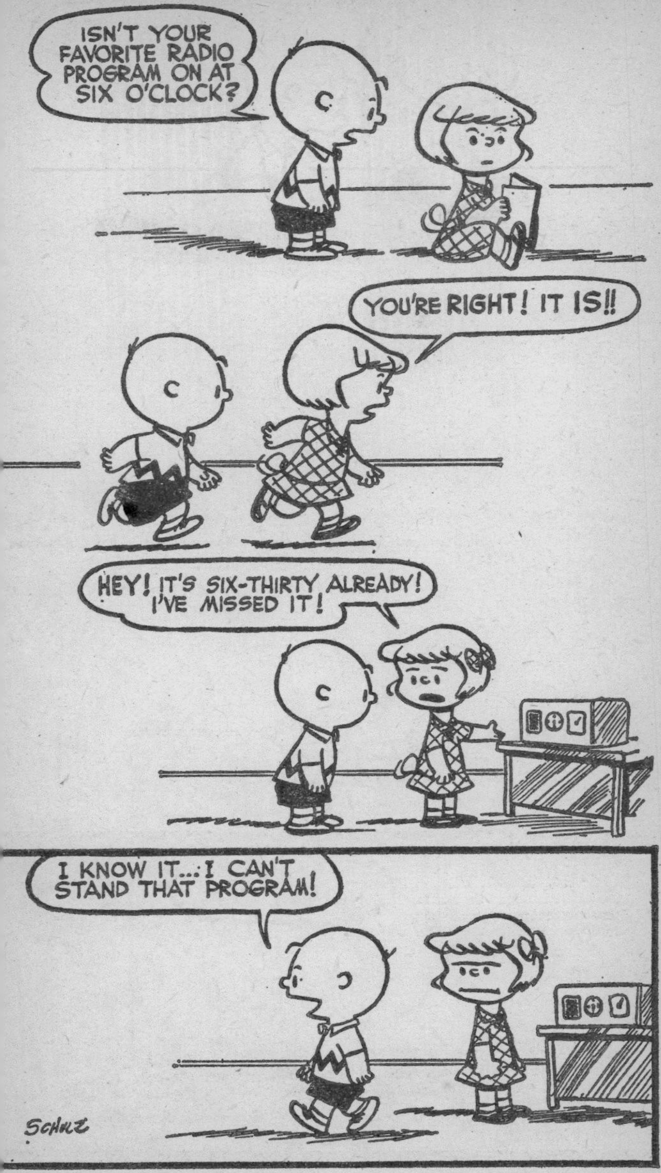

ISN'T YOUR FAVORITE RADIO PROGRAM ON AT SIX O'CLOCK?
YOU'RE RIGHT! IT IS!!
HEY! IT'S SIX-THIRTY ALREADY! I'VE MISSED IT!
I KNOW IT...I CAN'T STAND THAT PROGRAM!
SCHULZ

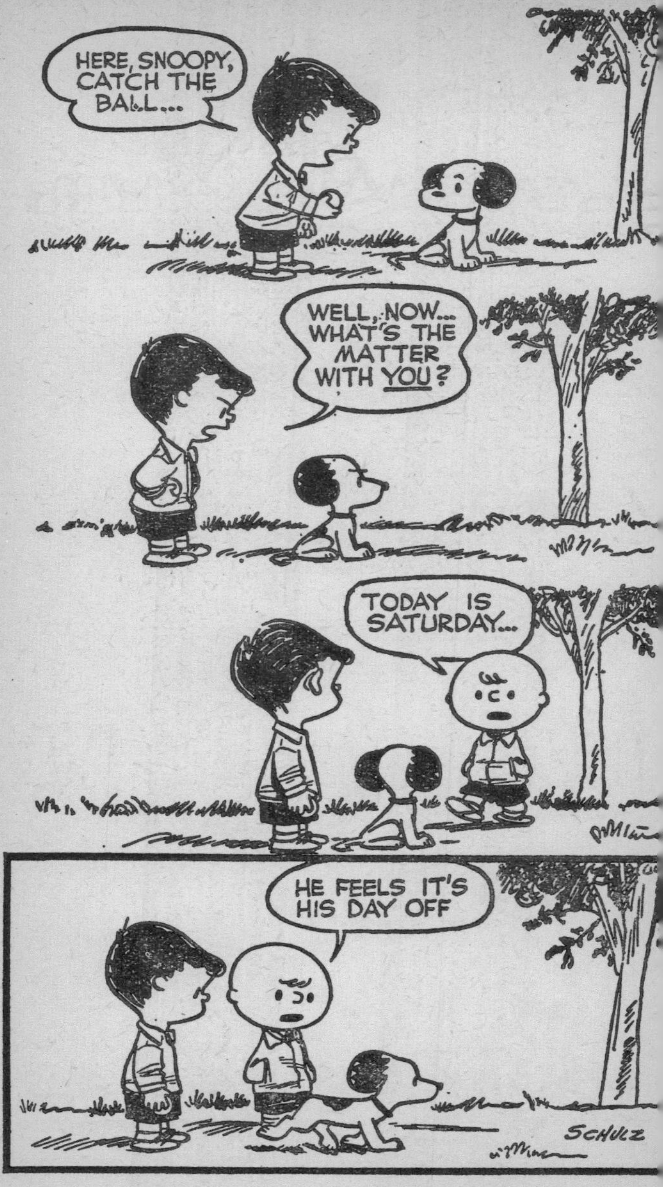
HERE, SNOOPY, CATCH THE BALL...
WELL, NOW... WHAT'S THE MATTER WITH YOU?
TODAY IS SATURDAY...
HE FEELS IT'S HIS DAY OFF
SCHULZ

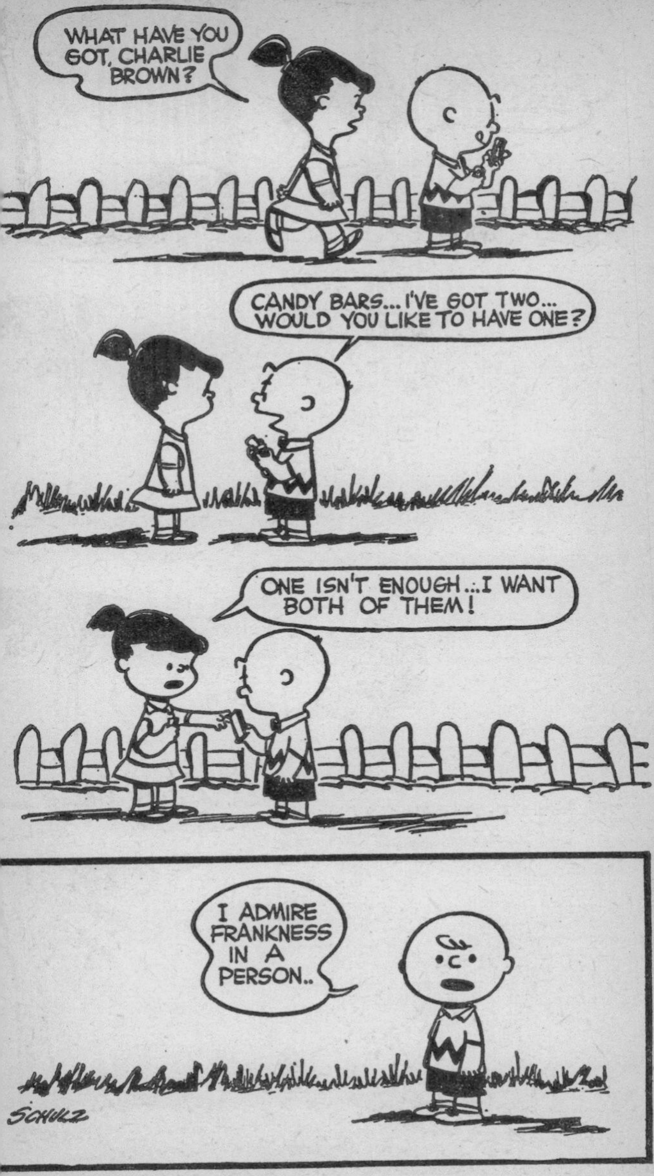
WHAT HAVE YOU GOT, CHARLIE BROWN?
CANDY BARS... I'VE GOT TWO... WOULD YOU LIKE TO HAVE ONE?
ONE ISN'T ENOUGH... I WANT BOTH OF THEM!
I ADMIRE FRANKNESS IN A PERSON..
SCHULZ

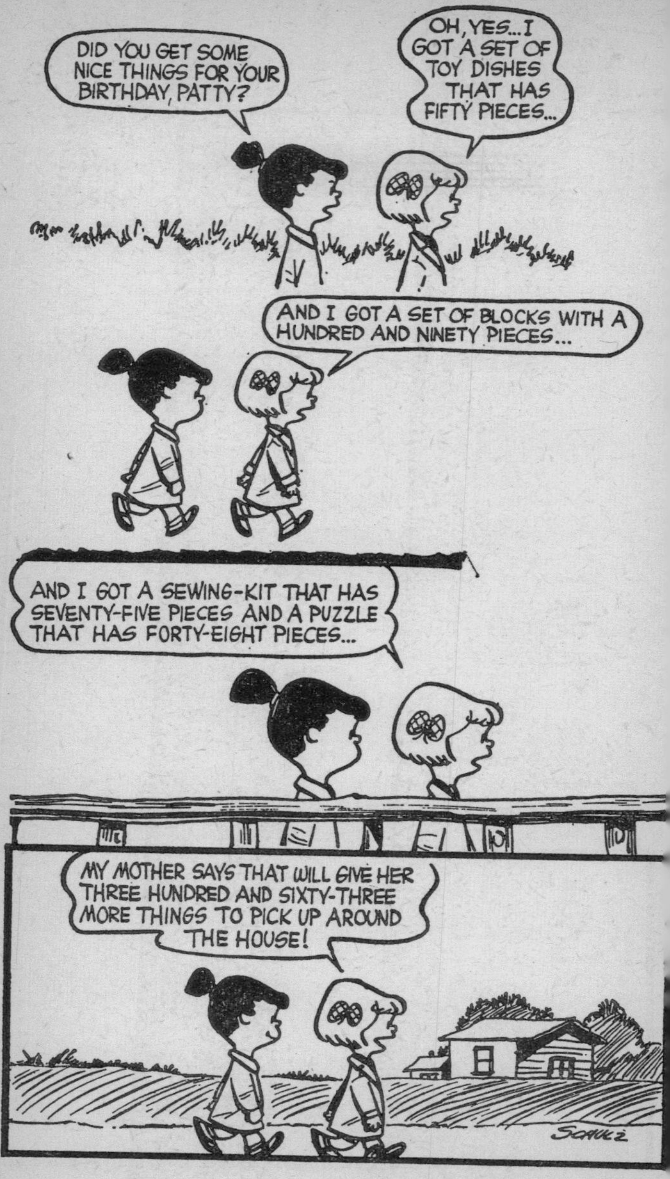
DID YOU GET SOME NICE THINGS FOR YOUR BIRTHDAY, PATTY?
OH, YES...I GOT A SET OF TOY DISHES THAT HAS FIFTY PIECES...
AND I GOT A SET OF BLOCKS WITH A HUNDRED AND NINETY PIECES...
AND I GOT A SEWING-KIT THAT HAS SEVENTY-FIVE PIECES AND A PUZZLE THAT HAS FORTY-EIGHT PIECES...
MY MOTHER SAYS THAT WILL GIVE HER THREE HUNDRED AND SIXTY-THREE MORE THINGS TO PICK UP AROUND THE HOUSE!
SCHULZ

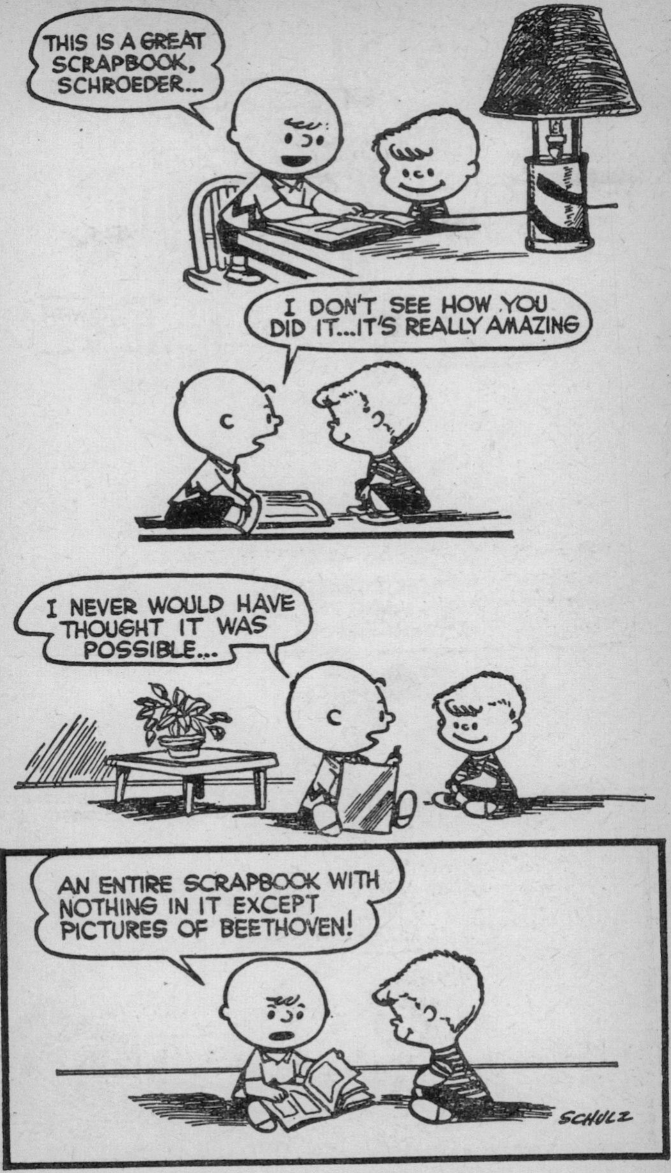
THIS IS A GREAT SCRAPBOOK, SCHROEDER...
I DON'T SEE HOW YOU DID IT...IT'S REALLY AMAZING
I NEVER WOULD HAVE THOUGHT IT WAS POSSIBLE...
AN ENTIRE SCRAPBOOK WITH NOTHING IN IT EXCEPT PICTURES OF BEETHOVEN!
SCHULZ

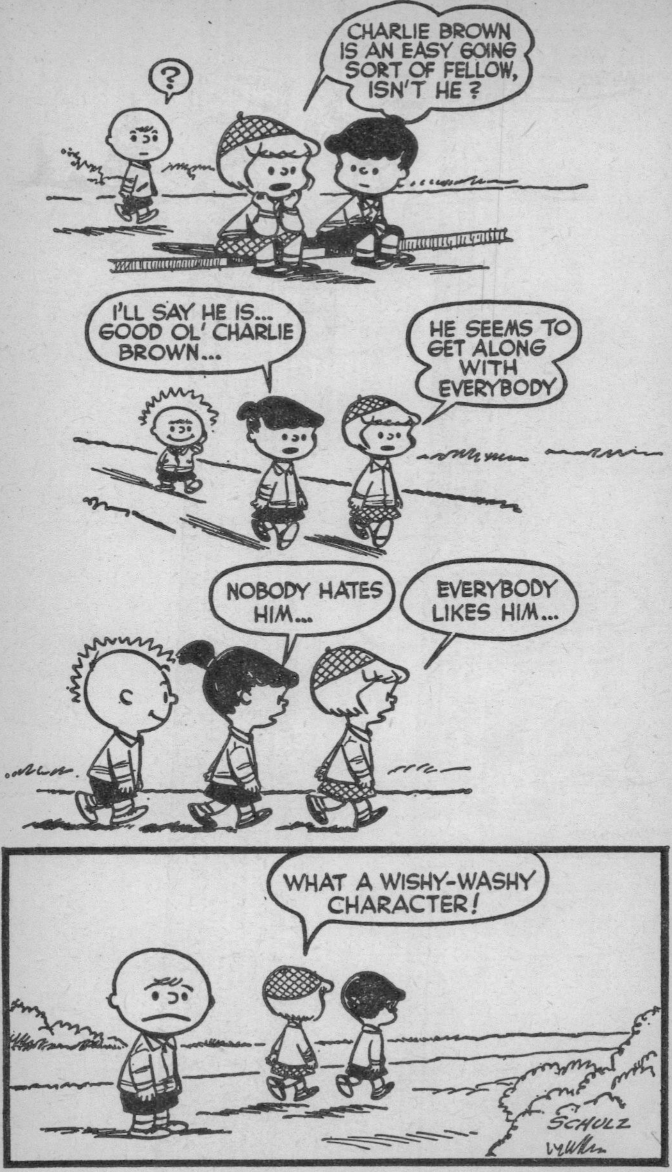
?
CHARLIE BROWN IS AN EASY GOING SORT OF FELLOW, ISN'T HE ?
I'LL SAY HE IS... GOOD OL' CHARLIE BROWN...
HE SEEMS TO GET ALONG WITH EVERYBODY
NOBODY HATES HIM...
EVERYBODY LIKES HIM...
WHAT A WISHY-WASHY CHARACTER!
SCHULZ

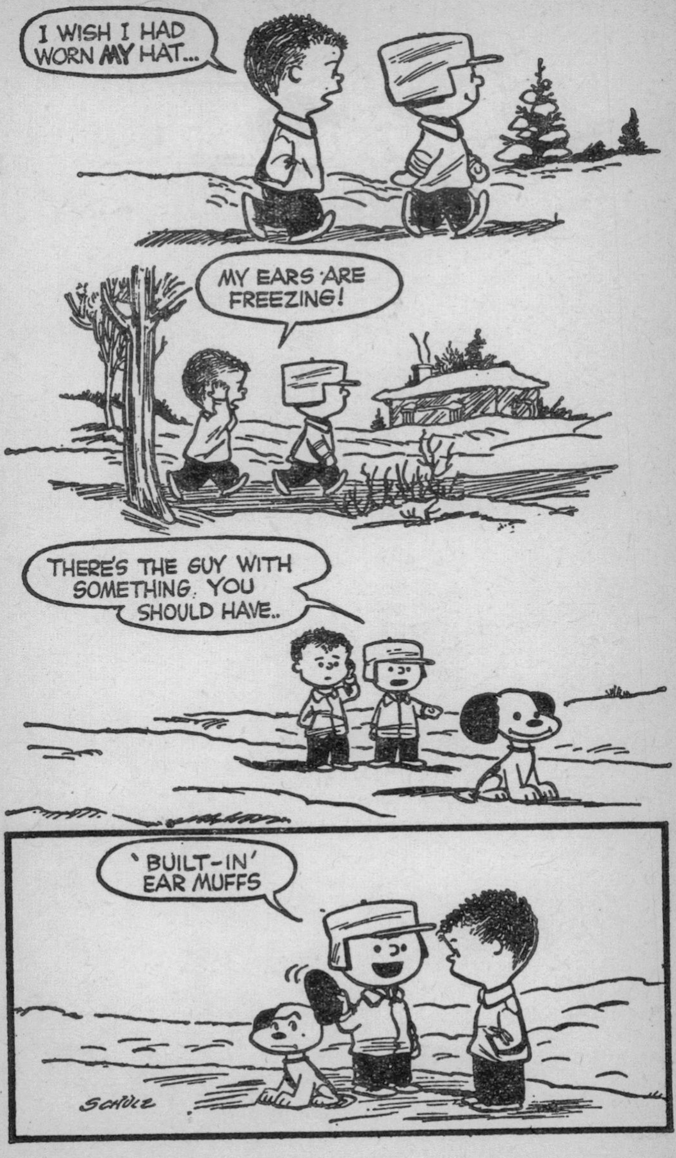
I WISH I HAD WORN MY HAT...
MY EARS ARE FREEZING!
THERE'S THE GUY WITH SOMETHING YOU SHOULD HAVE..
'BUILT-IN' EAR MUFFS
SCHULZ

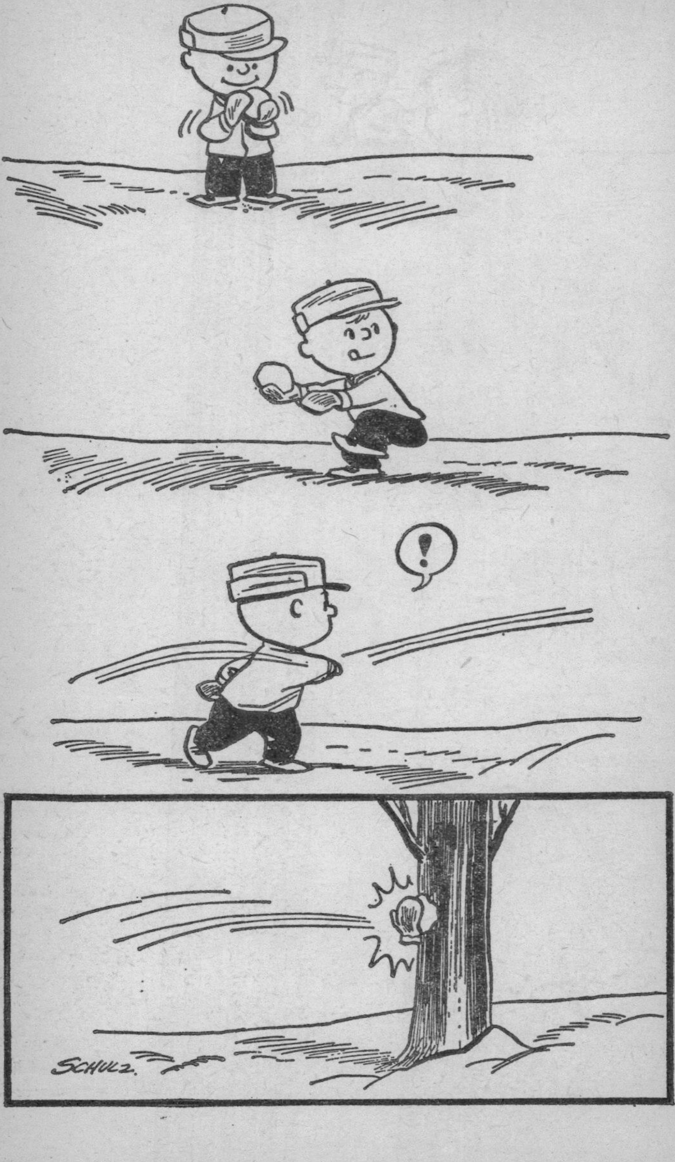
!
SCHULZ

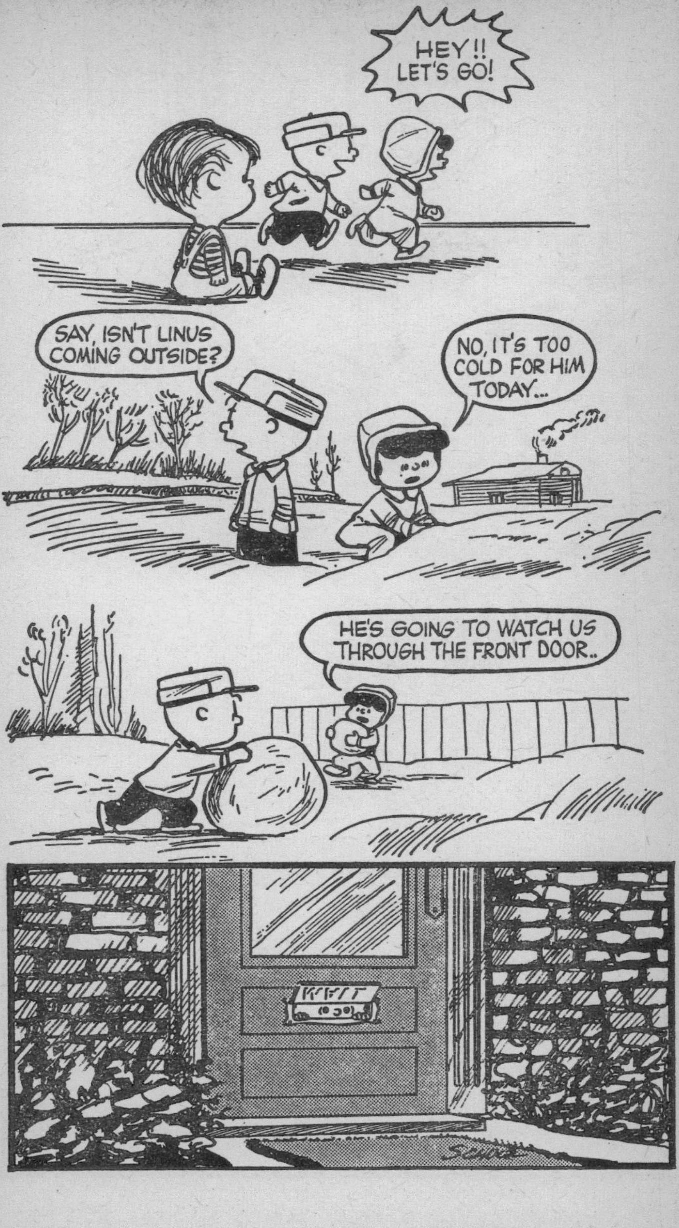

HEY!! LET'S GO!
SAY, ISN'T LINUS COMING OUTSIDE?
NO, IT'S TOO COLD FOR HIM TODAY...
HE'S GOING TO WATCH US THROUGH THE FRONT DOOR..

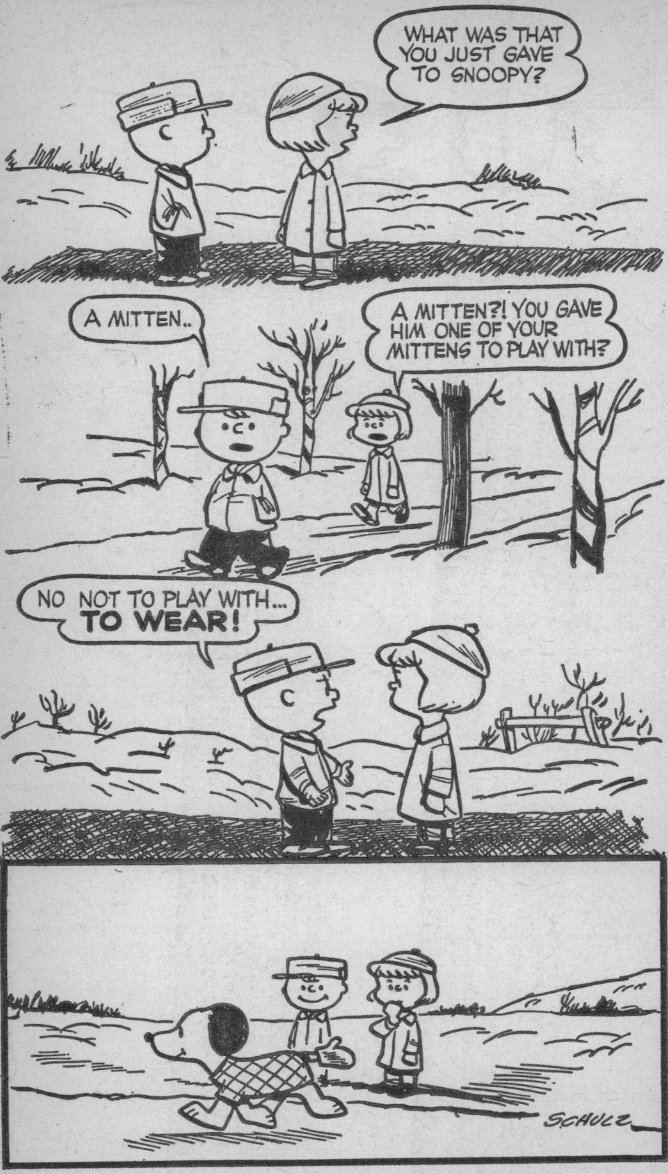
WHAT WAS THAT YOU JUST GAVE TO SNOOPY?
A MITTEN..
A MITTEN?! YOU GAVE HIM ONE OF YOUR MITTENS TO PLAY WITH?
NO NOT TO PLAY WITH... TO WEAR!
SCHULZ

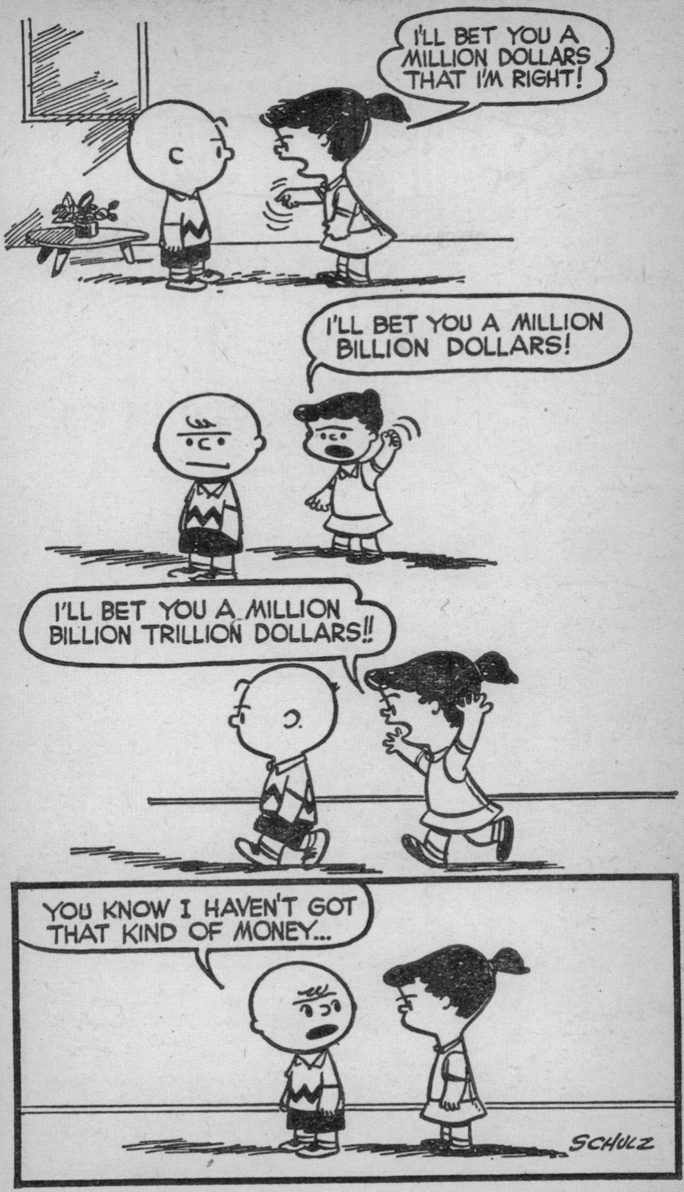
I'LL BET YOU A MILLION DOLLARS THAT I'M RIGHT!
I'LL BET YOU A MILLION BILLION DOLLARS!
I'LL BET YOU A MILLION BILLION TRILLION DOLLARS!!
YOU KNOW I HAVEN'T GOT THAT KIND OF MONEY...
SCHULZ

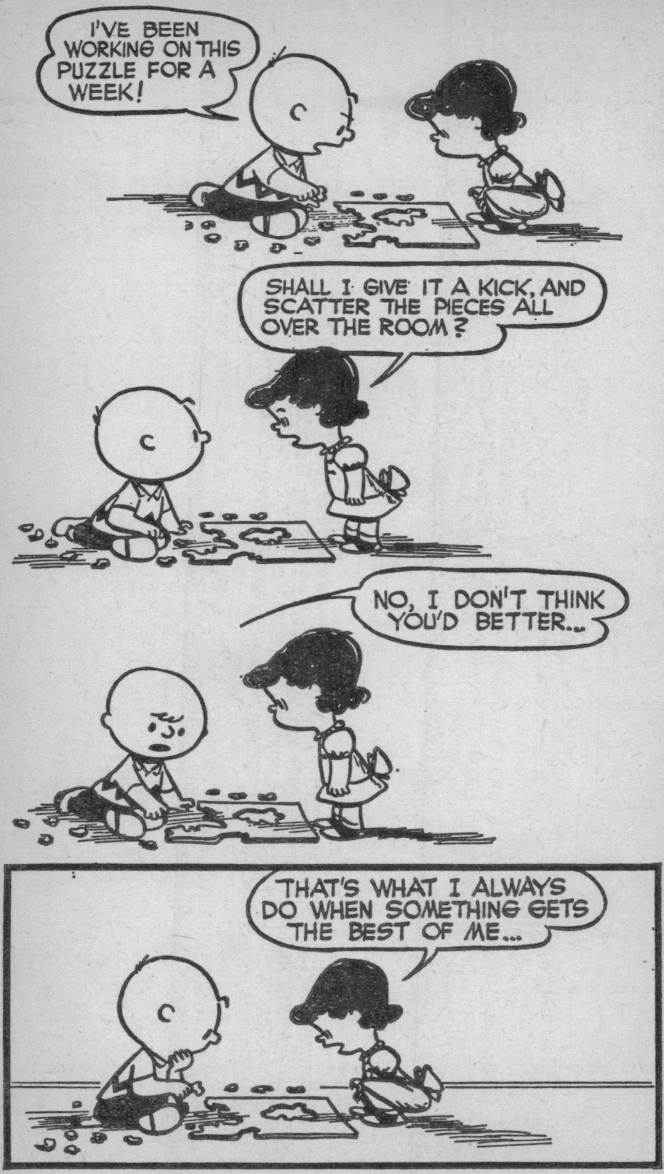
I'VE BEEN WORKING ON THIS PUZZLE FOR A WEEK!
SHALL I GIVE IT A KICK, AND SCATTER THE PIECES ALL OVER THE ROOM?
NO, I DON'T THINK YOU'D BETTER...
THAT'S WHAT I ALWAYS DO WHEN SOMETHING GETS THE BEST OF ME...

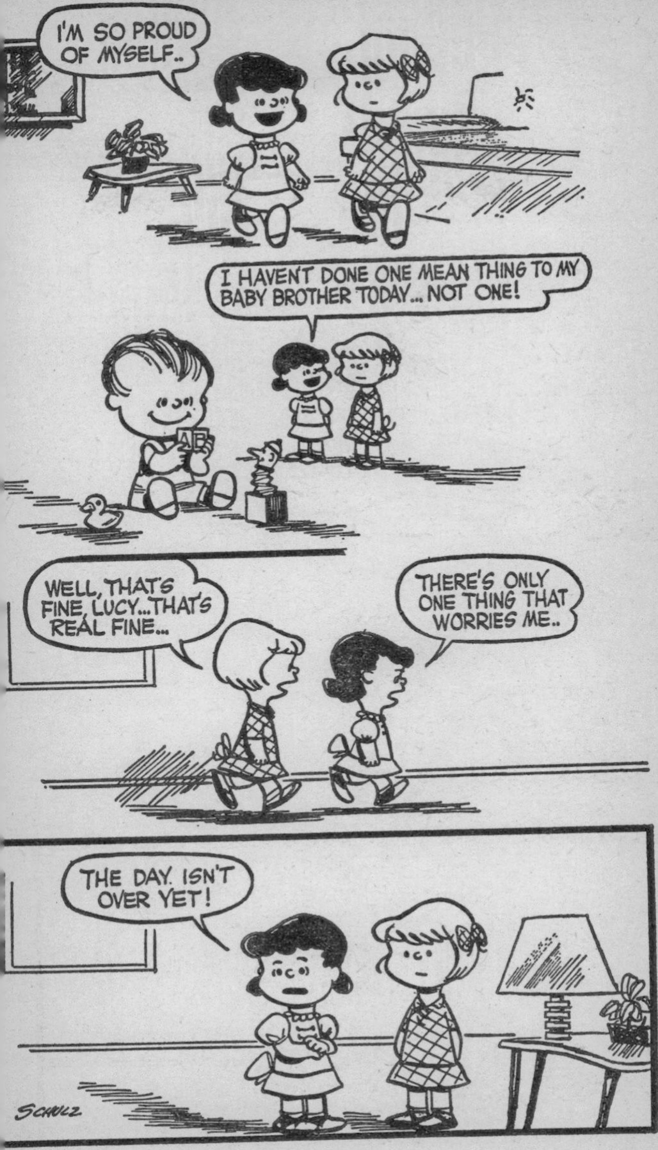
I'M SO PROUD OF MYSELF..
I HAVEN'T DONE ONE MEAN THING TO MY BABY BROTHER TODAY... NOT ONE!
AB
WELL, THAT'S FINE, LUCY...THAT'S REAL FINE...
THERE'S ONLY ONE THING THAT WORRIES ME..
THE DAY ISN'T OVER YET!
SCHULZ

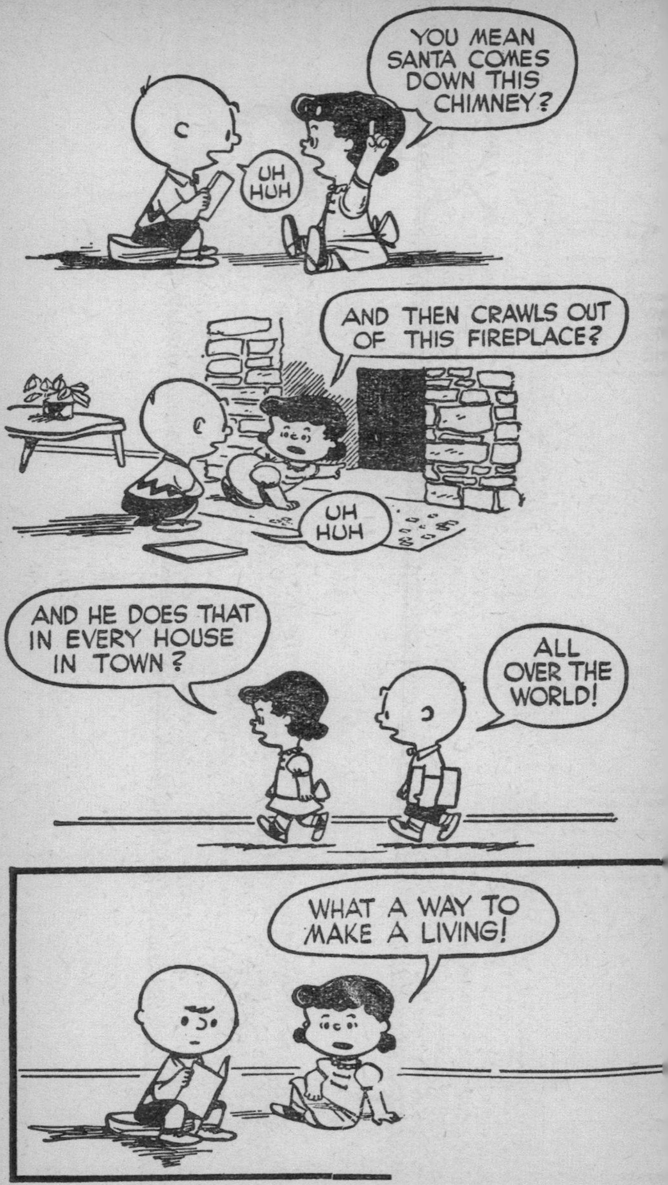
YOU MEAN SANTA COMES DOWN THIS CHIMNEY?
UH HUH
AND THEN CRAWLS OUT OF THIS FIREPLACE?
UH HUH
AND HE DOES THAT IN EVERY HOUSE IN TOWN?
ALL OVER THE WORLD!
WHAT A WAY TO MAKE A LIVING!

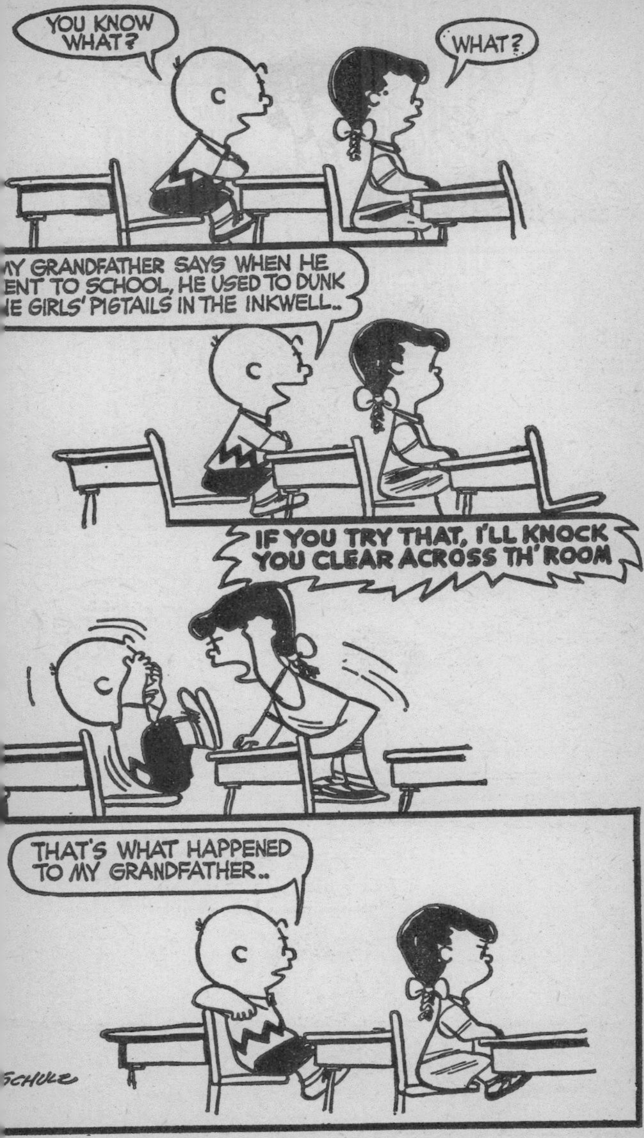
YOU KNOW WHAT?
WHAT?
MY GRANDFATHER SAYS WHEN HE
ENT TO SCHOOL, HE USED TO DUNK
E GIRLS' PIGTAILS IN THE INKWELL..
IF YOU TRY THAT, I'LL KNOCK YOU CLEAR ACROSS TH' ROOM
THAT'S WHAT HAPPENED TO MY GRANDFATHER..

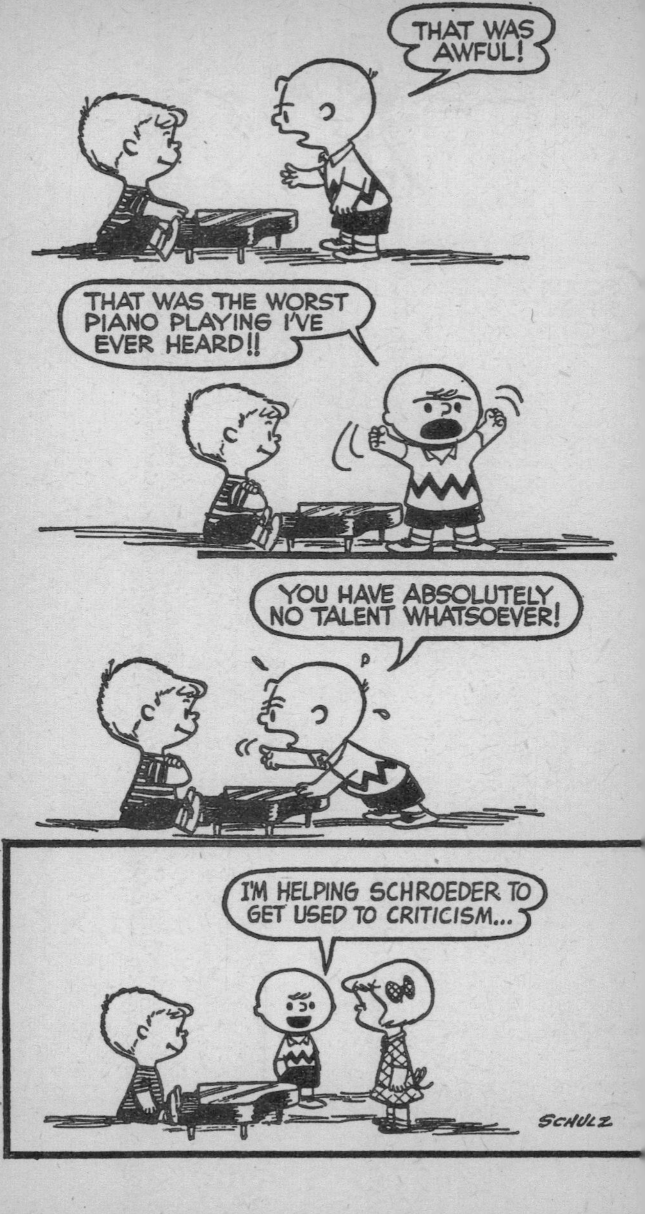

THAT WAS AWFUL!
THAT WAS THE WORST PIANO PLAYING I'VE EVER HEARD!!
YOU HAVE ABSOLUTELY NO TALENT WHATSOEVER!
I'M HELPING SCHROEDER TO GET USED TO CRITICISM...
SCHULZ

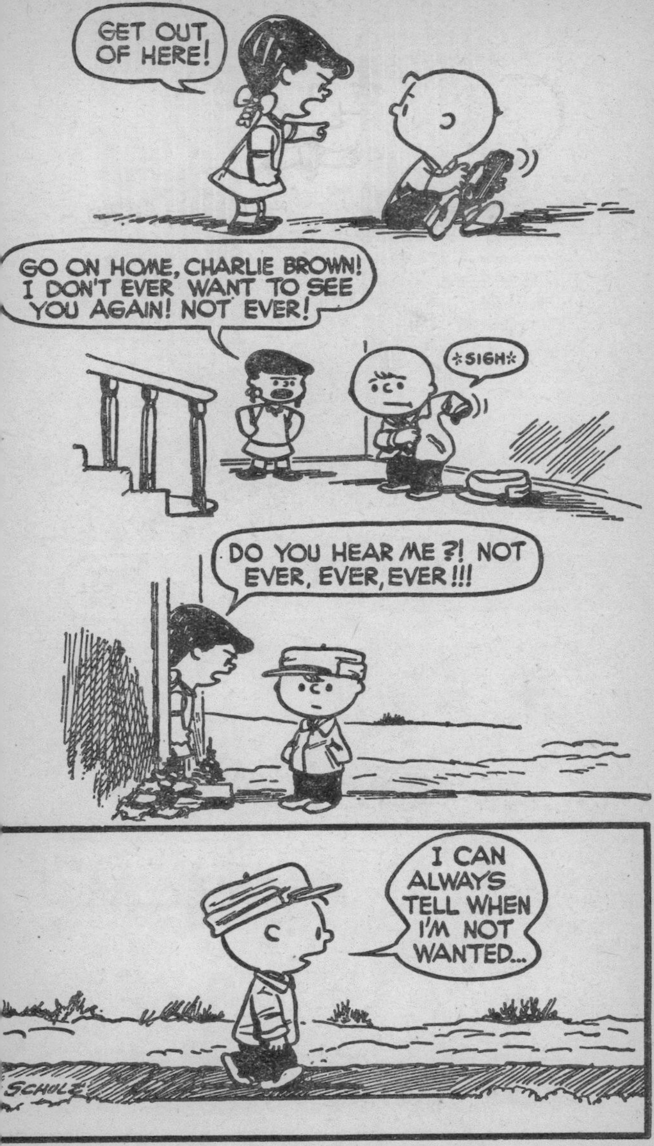
GET OUT OF HERE!
GO ON HOME, CHARLIE BROWN! I DON'T EVER WANT TO SEE YOU AGAIN! NOT EVER!
SIGH
DO YOU HEAR ME ?! NOT EVER, EVER, EVER!!!
I CAN ALWAYS TELL WHEN I'M NOT WANTED...
SCHULZ

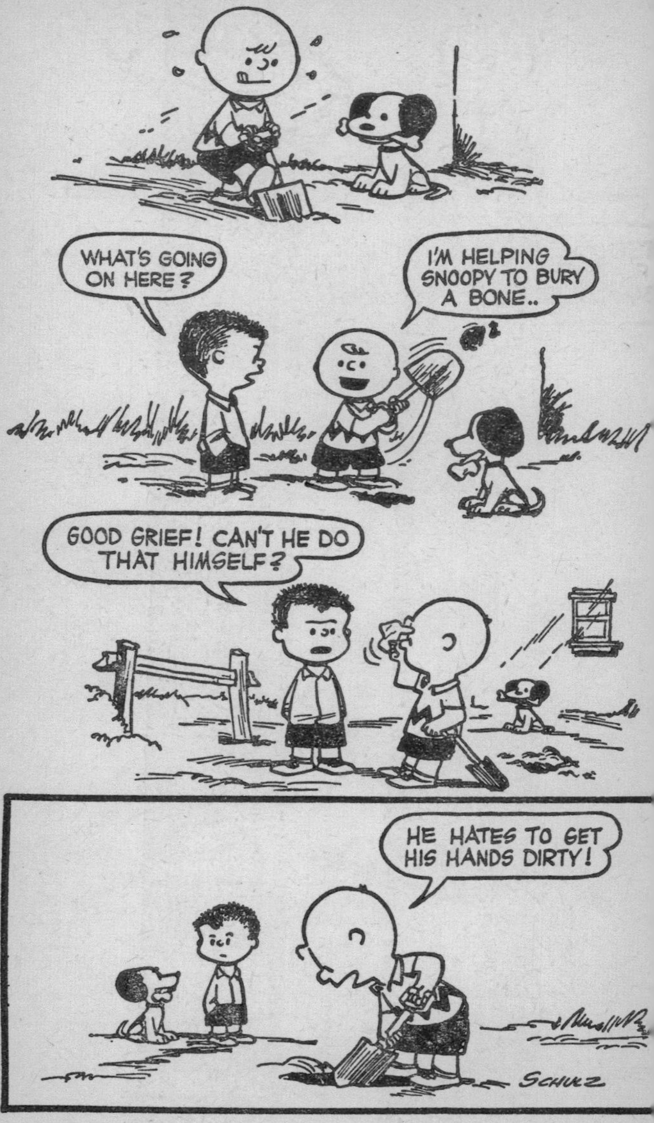
WHAT'S GOING ON HERE?
I'M HELPING SNOOPY TO BURY A BONE..
GOOD GRIEF! CAN'T HE DO THAT HIMSELF?
HE HATES TO GET HIS HANDS DIRTY!
SCHULZ

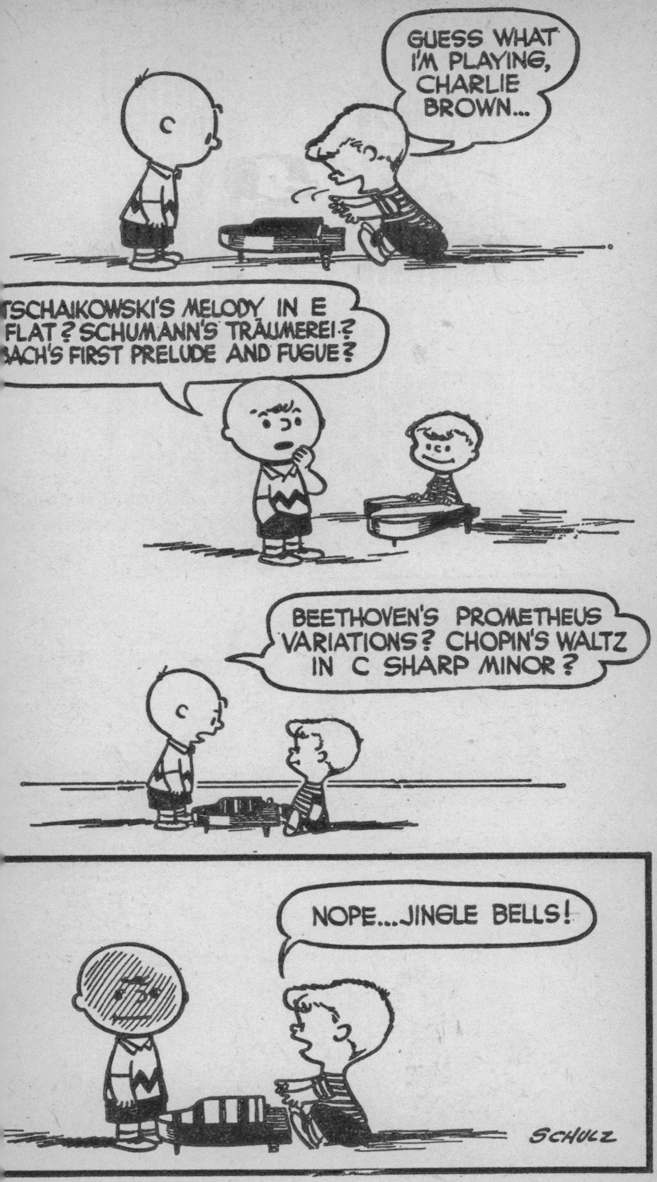
GUESS WHAT I'M PLAYING, CHARLIE BROWN...
TSCHAIKOWSKI'S MELODY IN E FLAT? SCHUMANN'S TRÄUMEREI? ACH'S FIRST PRELUDE AND FUGUE?
BEETHOVEN'S PROMETHEUS VARIATIONS? CHOPIN'S WALTZ IN C SHARP MINOR?
NOPE....JINGLE BELLS!
SCHULZ

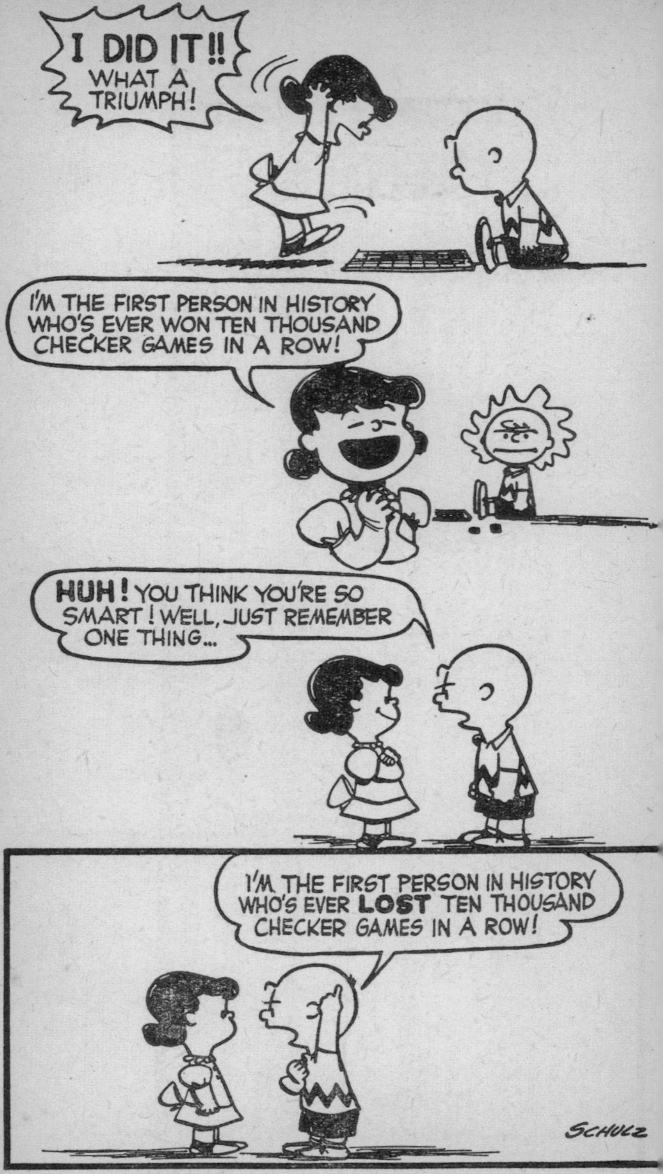
I DID IT!! WHAT A TRIUMPH!
I'M THE FIRST PERSON IN HISTORY WHO'S EVER WON TEN THOUSAND CHECKER GAMES IN A ROW!
HUH! YOU THINK YOU'RE SO SMART! WELL, JUST REMEMBER ONE THING...
I'M THE FIRST PERSON IN HISTORY WHO'S EVER LOST TEN THOUSAND CHECKER GAMES IN A ROW!
SCHULZ

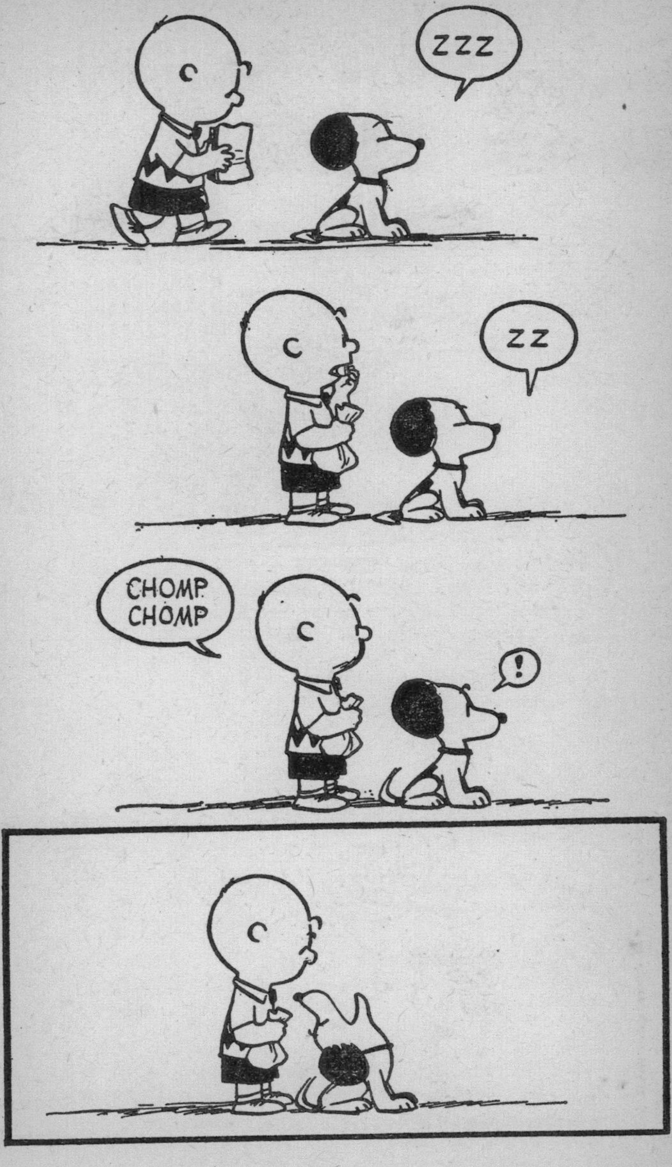
ZZZ
ZZ
CHOMP CHOMP
!

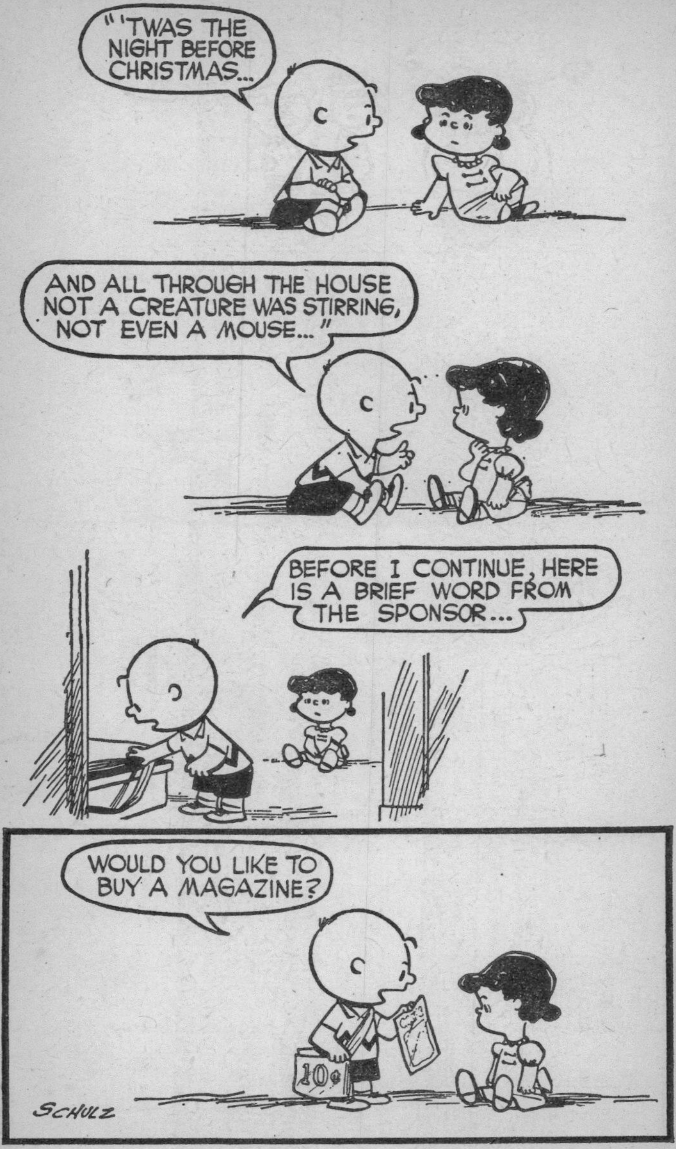
"'TWAS THE NIGHT BEFORE CHRISTMAS...
AND ALL THROUGH THE HOUSE NOT A CREATURE WAS STIRRING, NOT EVEN A MOUSE..."
BEFORE I CONTINUE, HERE IS A BRIEF WORD FROM THE SPONSOR...
WOULD YOU LIKE TO BUY A MAGAZINE?
10¢
SCHULZ

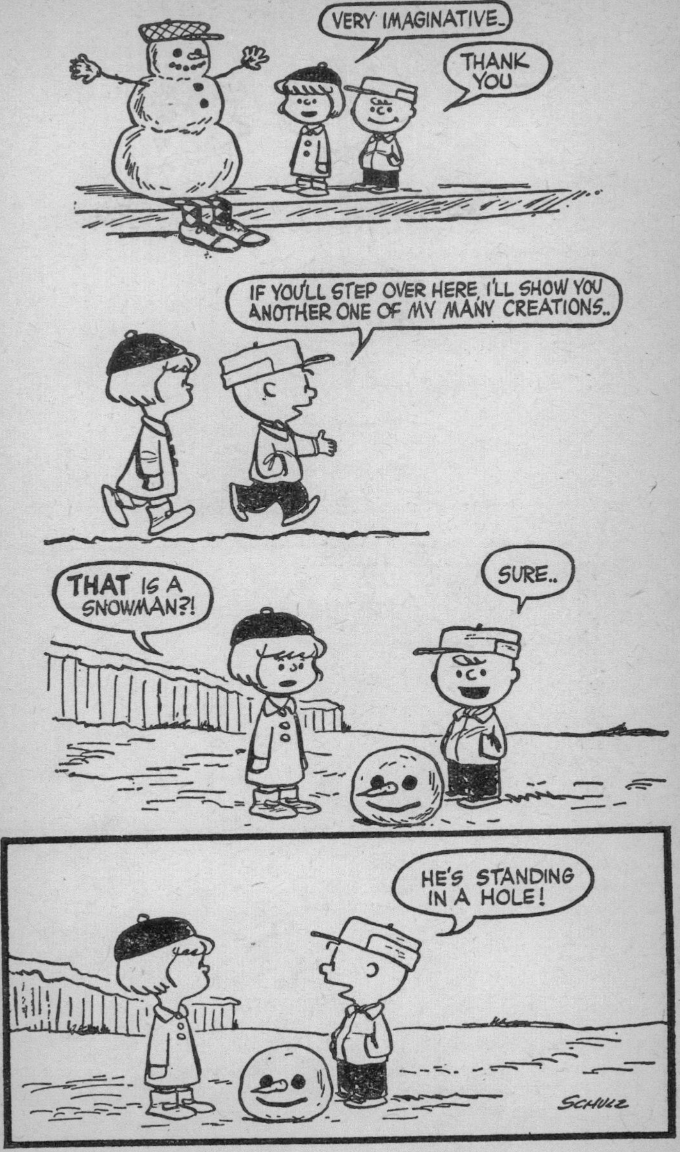
VERY IMAGINATIVE..
THANK YOU
IF YOU'LL STEP OVER HERE, I'LL SHOW YOU ANOTHER ONE OF MY MANY CREATIONS..
THAT IS A SNOWMAN?!
SURE..
HE'S STANDING IN A HOLE!
SCHULZ

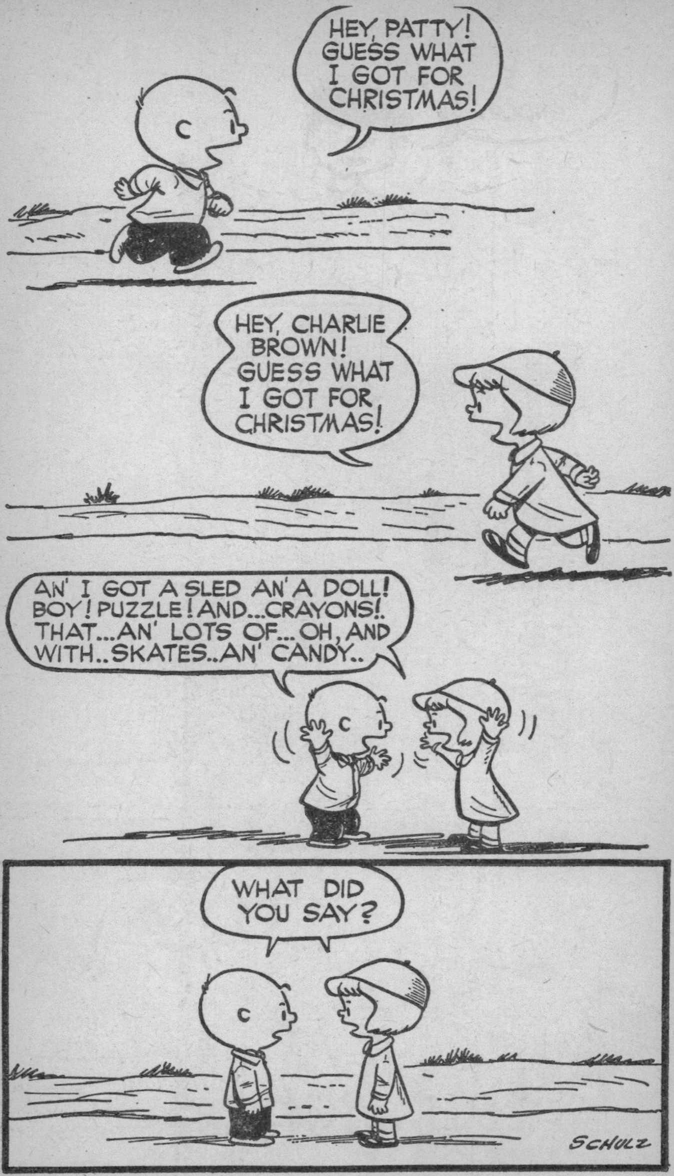
HEY, PATTY! GUESS WHAT I GOT FOR CHRISTMAS!
HEY, CHARLIE BROWN! GUESS WHAT I GOT FOR CHRISTMAS!
AN' I GOT A SLED AN' A DOLL! BOY! PUZZLE! AND...CRAYONS!. THAT...AN' LOTS OF...OH, AND WITH..SKATES..AN' CANDY..
WHAT DID YOU SAY?
SCHULZ

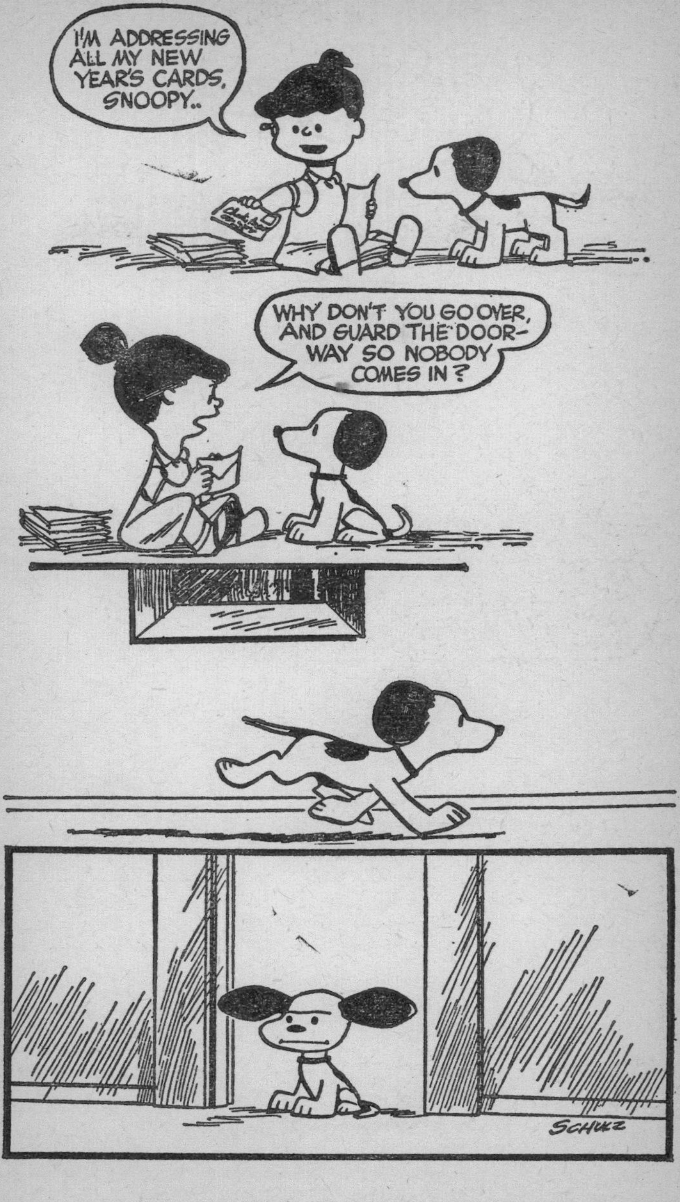
I'M ADDRESSING ALL MY NEW YEAR'S CARDS, SNOOPY..
WHY DON'T YOU GO OVER, AND GUARD THE DOORWAY SO NOBODY COMES IN?
SCHULZ

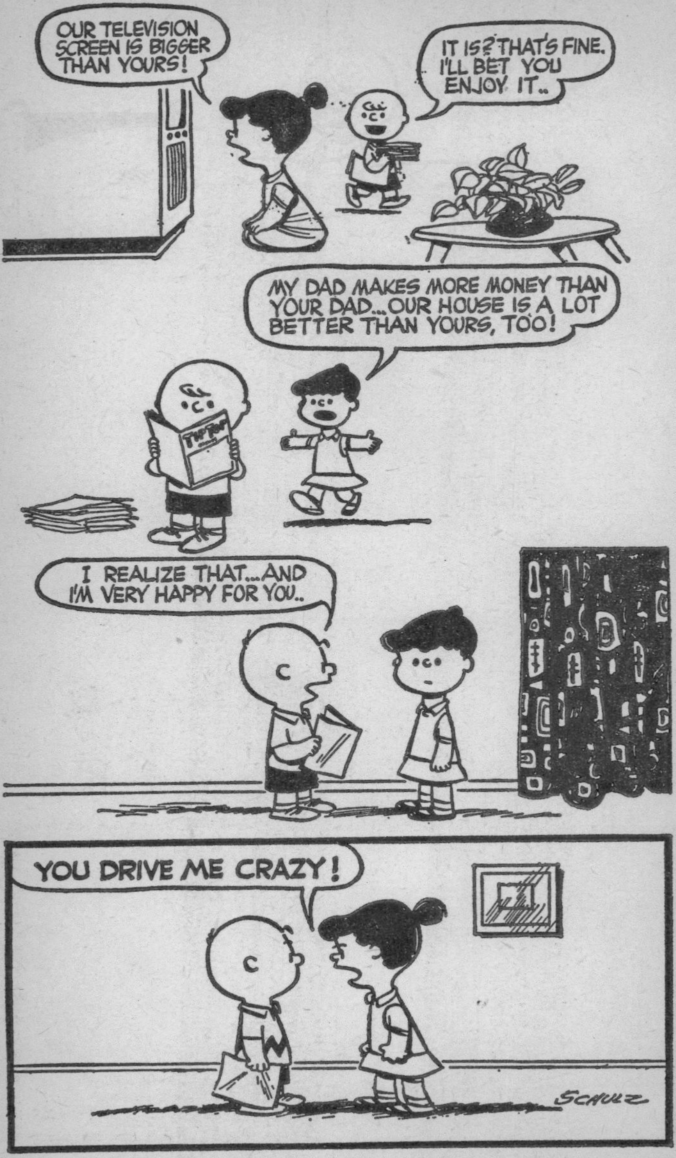
OUR TELEVISION SCREEN IS BIGGER THAN YOURS!
IT IS? THAT'S FINE. I'LL BET YOU ENJOY IT..
MY DAD MAKES MORE MONEY THAN YOUR DAD...OUR HOUSE IS A LOT BETTER THAN YOURS, TOO!
I REALIZE THAT...AND I'M VERY HAPPY FOR YOU..
YOU DRIVE ME CRAZY!
SCHULZ

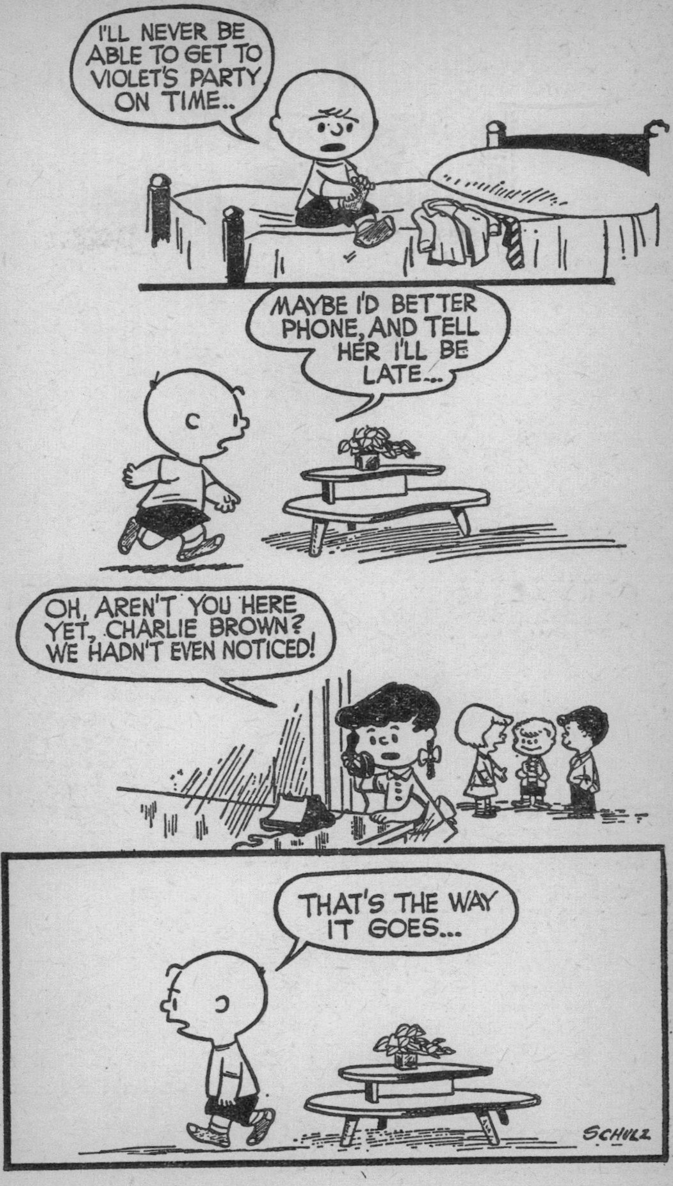

I'LL NEVER BE ABLE TO GET TO VIOLET'S PARTY ON TIME..
MAYBE I'D BETTER PHONE, AND TELL HER I'LL BE LATE...
OH, AREN'T YOU HERE YET, CHARLIE BROWN? WE HADN'T EVEN NOTICED!
THAT'S THE WAY IT GOES...
SCHULZ

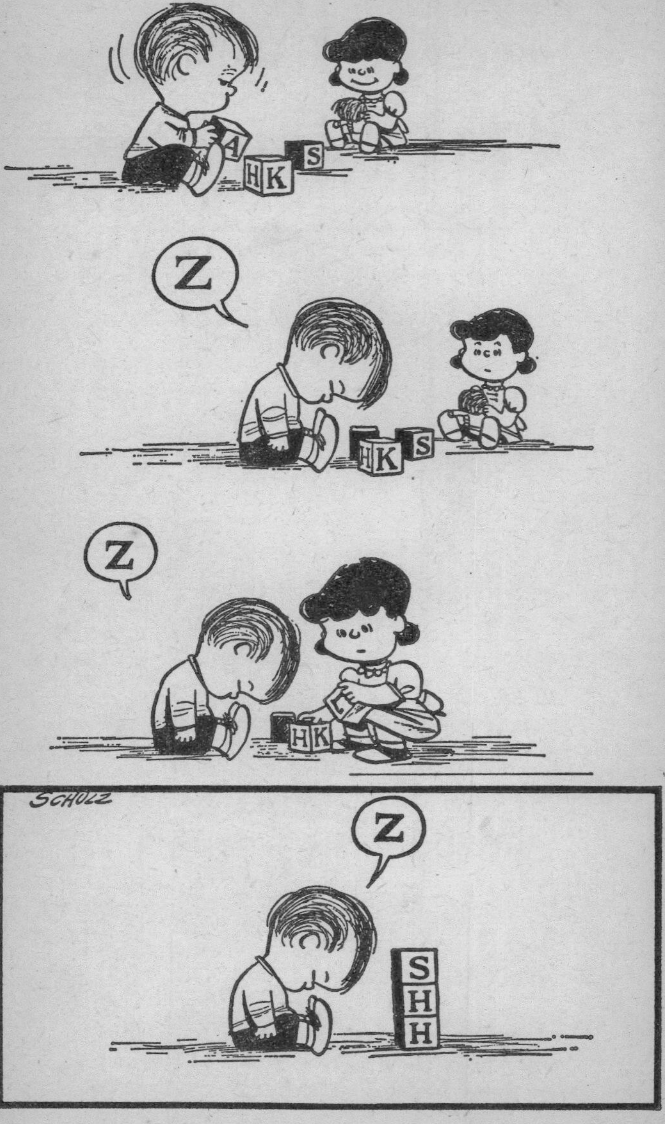
Z
Z
SCHULZ
Z
SHH